Sophia Smith

A Complete Genealogy of the Descendants of Matthew Smith of East Haddam

Sophia Smith

A Complete Genealogy of the Descendants of Matthew Smith of East Haddam

ISBN/EAN: 9783337399139

Printed in Europe, USA, Canada, Australia, Japan

Cover: Foto ©ninafisch / pixelio.de

More available books at **www.hansebooks.com**

A COMPLETE GENEALOGY

OF THE DESCENDANTS OF

MATTHEW SMITH

OF

EAST HADDAM, CONN.,

WITH MENTION OF HIS ANCESTORS.

1637—1890.

BY MRS. SOPHIA (SMITH) MARTIN,
HARTFORD, CONN.

RUTLAND:
THE TUTTLE COMPANY, PRINTERS.
1890.

INTRODUCTION.

The desire to know something of my ancestors, led me, in 1879, to compile "The Descendants of Col. David Mack" (there being already published Root and Ward genealogies), and to commence collecting material for a Smith genealogy; and I have now undertaken to preserve, in a valuable form, a record of the descendants of Matthew Smith from 1637 to 1890, the past 150 years being practically complete. Probably no work of this nature was ever published without errors of some kind, and I would consider it a favor to be informed of any.

The labor involved in this volume can be conceived of only by those who have undertaken a similar work, and especially is the name of *Smith* a difficult one. In the old records the name is spelled Smith, Smithe, Smeith and Smyth. It is one of the very oldest surnames, giving precedence to none, unless it be King.

There is no doubt that the ancestors were of English origin, and the Matthew which I have designated as 1st came to America from England in 1637, and in *direct descent* there appear *nine* by that name *alone*, the ninth dying unmarried.

Matthew 4th had a son, Thomas, who had sons, Thomas, Matthew and Samuel, and in *that* line it is possible there are some that bear that name.

I would make grateful acknowledgment to *all* who have contributed to this work, and would especially mention: Parsons P. Meacham, Meridian, N. Y.; Alden Smith, East Haddam, Conn.; Rev. H. W. Read, El Paso, Texas; Mrs. Anna M. Dinsmore, Portland, Mich.

In reference to this volume,

"Don't view me with a critic's eye,
But pass my imperfections by."

Mrs. Sophia (Smith) Martin.

Hartford, Conn., 1890.

GENEALOGY.

1st.

Matthew Smith, a cordwainer (a shoemaker), came from Sandwich, County of Kent, England, in 1637, with his wife, Jane and four children, and was said to have been admitted inhabitant of Charlestown, Mass., the same year. His wife became a member of the church Oct. 22, 1639, and he in May, 1643. The names of the children could not be ascertained. In 1658, he was a householder, under the title of Good-man. The time of the death of Matthew and Jane does not appear.

2d.

Matthew Smith of Woburn, Mass., *undoubtedly* son of Matthew of Charlestown, Mass., was born in England and had seven children.

CHILDREN:

I. Eliza, b. Sept. 15, 1658.
II. Matthew, b. Sept. 2, 1659.
III. John, b. June 16, 1661, and died young.
IV. Samuel, b. April 29, 1662, and died young.
V. Samuel, b. July 26, 1663.
VI. Hannah, b. Oct. 21, 1664.
VII. John, b. Mar. 28, 1667.

3d.

Matthew 3d, son of Matthew 2d, grandson of Matthew 1st, b. Sept. 2, 1659; m. March 2, 1682, or June 20, 1684, Mary Cutler (daughter of John Cutler), who was b. Mar. 5, 1663, in Woburn, Mass., and had at least four children.

CHILDREN:

I. Matthew, b. in 1684, in Lyme, Conn.
II. Thomas.
III. Mary.
IV. Elizabeth.

Matthew and Thomas settled at Mt. Parnassus, in the central part of East Haddam, Conn., about 1706, each receiving a deed of a tract of land of Rev. Stephen Hosmer, bearing date Oct. 14, 1708, which was the beginning of the "Smith Homestead." Thomas, in 1708 or 1709, enlisted to go on an expedition to Albany, N. Y., to make the quota of Connecticut, 350 men, required for the reduction of the French. Ninety of the number never returned, Thomas being one of them.

Elizabeth married Thomas Hungerford, and lived on a farm by the Eight Mile river, in East Haddam, Conn. Mary was unmarried, as appears by the following agreement:

COPY.

BE IT KNOWN TO ALL TO WHOM IT MAY CONCERN:—We, Thomas Hungerford, and Elizabeth Hungerford, my wife, and Mary Smith, all of Haddam, on the east side of the great river, in ye County of Hartford and colony of Connecticut, for ourselves, our heirs, executors, administrators and assigns, do hereby mutually agree with our loving brother, Matthew Smith, of the town and county aforesaid, concerning ye distribution of ye estate of our brother, Thomas Smith, late of said Haddam, deceased, that is to say, he, the said Matthew Smith, is to pay all the just debts due from said estate, and to enjoy the lands belonging to ye estate of ye said Thomas Smith, deceased, as his own inheritance, to him, the said Matthew Smith, his heirs and assigns forever: the remainder of the estate to be divided after the following method: Ye said Matthew Smith is to have one undivided or half part of the movables to his own proper use and behoof forever: ye said Thomas and Elizabeth Hungerford and said Mary Smith are to have the other half of ye movable estate of ye said Thomas Smith, deceased, equally divided between them, upon the receipt whereof we, the said Thomas Hungerford, Elizabeth my wife, and Mary Smith, do hereby engage fully and wholly to acquit and discharge ye said Matthew Smith, his heirs and assigns forever; and, whereas, the said Thomas Smith was out in the late expedition to Albany, the said Matthew Smith is to take care to get his wages, and it is to be divided in the same manner with the rest of ye movables, they all bearing an equal share in the charges.

In witness whereof, we, the said parties above named, have hereunto set our hands, this 25th day of November, A. D. 1709.

his
THOMAS x HUNGERFORD.
mark.

ELIZABETH HUNGERFORD.

her
MARY x SMITH.
mark.

MATTHEW SMITH.

WITNESSES :—JOHN BOOGE, WILLIAM SPENCER.

Descendants of Matthew Smith, 4th.

4TH.

Matthew 4th, son of Matthew 3d, grandson of Matthew 2d, b. in 1684, in Lyme, Conn., m. Nov. 28, 1706, Sarah Mack, who was b. in 1684, and was sister of Josiah Mack, ancestor of Col. David Mack, "The Faithful Steward." He d. Dec. 6, 1751. She d. Jan. 18, 1755.

Matthew 4th came to East Haddam, Conn., the 6th day of Nov., 1706, and built a dwelling house on the tract of land purchased of Rev. Stephen Hosmer, which was occupied until 1778, when the present house was built by his son, Matthew 5th, and thus this homestead has been in the family nearly two hundred years, and the present house, over a hundred years old, is a tall and stately mansion, overlooking all the dwellings in the valley. He was a tanner, and received a license, of which the following is a copy:

"At a County Court at Hartford, March ye 5th, 1705–6, this court grants liberty to Matthew Smith, now residing at Haddam, to set up and use the trade of tanning of leather, the court being certified of his skill and ability to manage that trade."

(True copy.)
    [Attest.]   CALEB HANLEY, Clerk.

COPY OF SETTLEMENT OF ESTATE.

At a Court of Probate, held at E. Haddam, Jan. 15, 1752, present: John Buckley, Esq., Judge, Gerard Cone of East Haddam was appointed guardian to four of his children, namely, Matthew, Nehemiah, Ruth and Sarah Cone, minors, and became bound accordingly, and ye heirs of Capt. Matthew Smith, late of East Haddam, deceased, appeared and established an agreement and acknowledged the same, which was accepted and ordered to be recorded.

    [Attest.]   THOMAS ADAMS, Clerk.

Articles of agreement made this 15th day of January, 1752, by and between Thomas Smith, Matthew Smith, Joseph Cone and Mary, his wife, Thomas Rogers and Sarah, his wife, for themselves and Gerard Cone, guardian to his children, viz.: Matthew, Nehemiah, Ruth and Sarah, by his wife Ruth, deceased, that was ye daughter of Capt. Matthew Smith, late of E. Haddam, deceased, and Josiah Arnold, guardian to children, Lydia, Elizabeth and Josiah, by Lydia, his wife, deceased, that was ye daughter of ye said deceased Capt. Smith, and Nehemiah Tracy and Susannah, his wife, for themselves, all of East Haddam, in ye county of Hartford and colony of Connecticut, in New England: Witnesseth, that whereas our honored father, Capt. Matthew Smith, aforesaid, is lately deceased, and having made one last will and testament for ye disposition of his estate, whereby ye same becomes liable to be distributed to and among ye heirs and legal representatives of ye said Capt. Smith, deceased, bind ye Thomas Smith, Matthew Smith, Joseph Cone and Mary, his wife, Thomas Rogers and Sarah, his wife, and Nehemiah Tracy and Susannah, his wife, and ye aforenamed children of Gerard Cone and Josiah Arnold, and that ye said deceased estate may be divided and settled in ye most equitable manner among the heirs and legal representatives above said, we ye persons above said, in our respective capacities have agreed that ye same shall be done in ye following manner: That our loving brothers, Thomas and Matthew Smith, shall take administration on said deceased estate, and shall cause a true and perfect inventory of said deceased estate, both real and personal, to be made by Capt. John Gates, Mr. Stephen Brainard and Capt. Aaron Skinner, all of Colchester, in ye county of Hartford, and that ye administrators shall pay all ye debts due from said deceased estate and receive all ye credits, and add the same to ye inventory, and then shall cause our honored mother's right of dower and power of thirds to be set out to her in said deceased estate, according to law, and all ye residue of said deceased estate, remaining in the administrators' hands shall be divided in ye following proportion to and among ye heirs and legal representatives of said deceased, by ye appraisers aforesaid; that is to say,

Item 1st.—To Thomas Smith, his heirs and assigns forever, $\frac{1}{4}$ part of said deceased estate, said $\frac{1}{4}$ part to be set out to him in ye real estate of said deceased.

Item 2d.—To Matthew Smith, his heirs and assigns forever, one $\frac{1}{4}$ part of said deceased estate, said $\frac{1}{4}$ part to be set out to him in the real estate of said deceased.

Item 3d.—To Joseph Cone and Mary, his wife, their heirs and assigns ferevor, $\frac{1}{5}$ part of ye $\frac{1}{2}$ of said deceased estate.

Item 4th.—To Thomas Rogers and Sarah, his wife, their heirs and assigns forever, $\frac{1}{5}$ part of ye $\frac{1}{2}$ of said deceased estate.

Item 5th.—To ye heirs of Ruth Cone (daughter of said deceased), their heirs and assigns forever, $\frac{1}{5}$ part of ye $\frac{1}{2}$ of ye said deceased estate.

Item 6th.—To ye heirs of Lydia Arnold (daughter of said deceased), their heirs and assigns forever, $\frac{1}{6}$ part of ye $\frac{1}{2}$ of said deceased estate.

Item 7th.—To Nehemiah Tracy and Susannah, his wife, their heirs and assigns forever, $\frac{1}{5}$ part of ye $\frac{1}{2}$ of said deceased estate,

Item 8th.—It is agreed that Thomas and Matthew Smith shall have their shares of ye said real estate set out to them in the two largest tracts, one in ye one of them and the other in ye other large tract, and that it be so laid to them as that ye other claimers or sharers in these two tracts shall not be hurt or discommoded. And it is further to be understood that if all the heirs of Ruth Cone (daughter of said deceased), should die and leave no issue, then that part of said deceased estate that shall be set out to said minors, shall be and belong to their guardian, he, Gerard Cone, his heirs and assigns forever, in confirmation of what is above and within written. We have hereunto set our hands and seals the day and year above written.

THOMAS SMITH. [SEAL.]
MATTHEW SMITH. [SEAL.]
THOMAS ROGERS. [SEAL.]
her
SARAH x ROGERS. [SEAL.]
mark.
JOSEPH CONE. [SEAL.].
MARY CONE. [SEAL.]
JERARD CONE. [SEAL.]
JOSIAH ARNOLD. [SEAL.]
NEHEMIAH TRACY. [SEAL.]
SUSANNA TRACY. [SEAL.]

ADDITIONAL ARTICLE.

Item.—We do agree that, whereas the said deceased Capt. Smith, in his lifetime, at sundry times had given certain small portions of his estate to some of his daughters, yet that in ye distribution of his estate according to ye above agreement, no regard shall be had to that, and nothing be brought into an account but what Capt. Smith owned and possessed in his own right at ye time of his death.

Signed, sealed and delivered in presence of above witnesses.

[Attest.] THOMAS ADAMS, Clerk.

Court of Probate, s. s., East Haddam, Jan. ye 15, A. D. 1752. Personally appeared Thomas Smith, Matthew Smith, Thomas Rogers and Sarah, his wife, Joseph Cone and Mary, his wife, Jared Cone, Nehemiah Tracy, Susanna, his wife, and acknowledged this instrument to be their free act and deed.

[Attest.] THOMAS ADAMS, Clerk.

Court of Probate, to wit, East Haddam, Feb. 4, 1752. Personally appeared Mr. Josiah Arnold, and acknowledged this instrument to be his free act and deed.

[Attest.] THOMAS ADAMS, Clerk.

The above is a true copy of the original document, as recorded in Vol. 2 of the Probate records in the district of Colchester.

[Attest.] ERASTUS DAY,
Judge of Probate.

CHILDREN : (of Matthew 4th.)

I. Thomas, b. Mar. 20, 1710.
II. Sarah, b. Feb. 21, 1711.
III. Mary, b. ——— 1713.
IV. Elizabeth, b. April 20, 1716, d. in 1741—unmarried.
V. Lydia, b. Feb. 24, 1718.
VI. Ruth, b. Mar 29, 1720.
VII. Matthew, b. Nov. 1, 1722.
VIII. Susanna, b. ——— 1725.

I.

Thomas, son of Matthew 4th, grandson of Matthew 3d, b. Mar. 26, 1710, m. 1st, Feb. 9, 1737, Hannah Gates, who was b. about 1714 and d. January 12, 1754; and he m. 2d, May 27, 1756, Mrs. Anna Osborne, widow of Dr. Osborne, who was b. about 1715 and d. April 16, 1791, and was buried in E. Haddam, Conn., in the graveyard near the "Smith Homestead." He d. Dec. 23, 1797, and was buried in the same graveyard.

CHILDREN: (1st marriage.)

I. Thomas, b. Jan. 21, 1738.
II. Matthew, b. Sept. 11, 1740.

(2d marriage.)

III. Samuel, b. Dec. 6, 1757.

Thomas m. Dec. 11, 1760, Mary Green of Middletown, Conn., and had six children, Benjamin, Jonah, Mary, Hannah, Diodate and Eliphalet, twins.

Matthew m. and had twelve children, six sons and six daughters. The names of the daughters were *Hannah*, who m. Stephen Fuller; *Lydia*, who m. Jabez Fuller; *Thankful*, who m. Irad Fuller; *Esther*, who m. Josiah Gates; *Olive*, who m. Jonas Sparks; *Dorothy*, who m. William Palmer.

II.

Sarah, dau. of Matthew 4th, gr. dau. of Matthew 3d, b. Feb. 21, 1711, m. April 19, 1746, Thomas Rogers. No record of his birth or death could be found. He did not die until after 1774. She d. Dec. 20, 1754.

CHILDREN:

I. John, b. Feb. 3, 1747.
II. Elizabeth, b. Mar. 19, 1750.
III. Mary, b. July 15, 1752.
IV. Thomas, Jr., b. Dec. 15, 1754.

Descendants of Mary Smith and Joseph Cone.

—:o:—

III.

Mary, dau. of Matthew 4th, gr. dau. of Matthew 3d, b. in 1713, m. Nov. 1, 1734, Joseph Cone, son of Daniel, Jr., who was b. Mar. 20, 1711. No record of death of either could be found.

CHILDREN:

I. Joseph, b. Nov. 2, 1735.
II. Mary, b. Mar. 27, 1738.
III. Benjamin, b. Sept. 20, 1739.
IV. Martin, b. May 15, 1742.
V. Martha, b. April 10, 1744.
VI. Solomon, b. Sept. 2, 1745.
VII. Ashbel, b. Aug. 2, 1747.
VIII. Jeremiah, b. Feb. 7, 1750.
IX. Elizabeth, b. Aug. 22, 1751.
X. Theodore, b. Aug. 12, 1758.

The following is all that has been found about each of the above, and is far from being complete, but is supposed to be correct as far as it descends.

Joseph Cone, son of Mary, gr. son of Matthew 4th, b. Mar. 2, 1735, m. June 14, 1759, Martha Spencer, who was b. in 1740, and d. May 3, 1796. He d. 1779. (?)

CHILDREN:

I. Conant, b. July 6, 1760, m. Alice Houghton, (dau. of Joab Houghton). Rev. Spencer Houghton Cone, D. D., of New York City, an eminent Baptist divine, was his son and was b. April 30, 1785, and m. May, 1813, Sally Wallace Morrell of Philadelphia. He was in Princeton College for a time, then a teacher, and in 1805 became an actor and played in Philadelphia and other cities with good success for seven years. Miss Morrell saw him on the stage and fell in love with him, but before she would marry him she required him to give up the stage, which he did and took an editorial position on a Baltimore newspaper. In 1814 he got an appointment in the treasury under Geo. M. Dallas, at the same time turning his attention to the pulpit and preaching in some churches in Washington and the neighborhood. In 1815–16 Congress made him chaplain, and in 1823 he was called to the Oliver St. Baptist church, New York City, and in 1841 he took charge of the Broome St. church, where he remained till his death, in 1855. During his entire ministry he was conspicuous in all branches of church work. He was a prominent divine in the Baptist denomination, which he divided by the introduction of his new version. He left a son, Spencer Wallace (Cone), who was a journalist and poet. He was colonel of the 61st Reg. N. Y. Vol., and d. at Larchmont Manor, at the house of his son-in-law, Chas. A. Stevenson. Mr. C.'s daughter, (Mrs. Stevenson) went on the stage and gained a reputation. She is best known as "Kate Claxton."

II. Alice, b. Feb. 18, 1762, m. a Mr. Sparrow. Both Alice and her brother Conant lived at their grandfather Spencer's after their father died. Conant was aid, in the Revolutionary war, for his gr. father, Joseph Cone.

III. Prudence.

IV. John.

V. Martha.

VI. Timothy, b. May 20, 1777, m. in 1806, Sarah Howard Bailey, who was b. in 1790. He d. in 1864. He alone lived with his mother, and when fourteen she took him to New Hampshire to learn the trade of millwright. When his time was out, at the age of twenty-one, he went to E. Haddam, expecting to find his mother there, but learned that she had been dead two years. Her brother, Dr. Joseph Spencer, lived in Lansingburgh, N. Y., and she went to visit him, but when she arrived there she found he had gone to Ohio, and it so preyed upon her mind that she became deranged and after awhile died. (All of Joseph and Martha's family suffered from insanity except Timothy.)

CHILDREN: (of Timothy Cone.)

I.—Deborah Packard, b. Feb. 25, 1808, d. April 15, 1863.
II.—Martha Spencer, b. Dec. 20, 1810, m. ——————— Blankinton.
III.—Mary, b. Mar. 17, 1813, now resides at Marietta, Ohio.
IV.—George, b. June 9, 1815, d. in 1883.
V.—Charles, b. Oct. 23, 1817.
VI.—Sarah, b. May 9, 1820, d. in 1871.
VII.—Joseph Spencer, b. Aug. 26, 1822.
VIII.—Timothy, b. Nov. 9, 1825, d. in 1887, unmarried.
IX.—Alice Sparrow, b. Nov. 17, 1827, and m. —— Brush.
X.—Ellen, b. Mar. 14, 1830, and m. H. A. Peck, and d. in 1862.

Mary Cone, dau. of Mary, gr. dau. of Matthew 4th, was b Mar. 27, 1738, and m. David Emmons.

Benjamin Cone, son of Mary, gr. son of Matthew 4th, was b. Sept. 20, 1739, and d. Oct. 16, 1758.

Martin Cone, son of Mary, gr. son of Matthew 4th, was b. May 15, 1742, m. June 5, 1764, Rebecca Spencer, who d. July 3, 1785.

Martha Cone, dau. of Mary, gr. dau. of Matthew 4th, was b. April 10, 1744, and m. Levi Beebe, a revolutionary soldier.

Solomon Cone, son of Mary, gr. son of Matthew 4th, b. Sept. 2, 1745, m. May 30, 1774, Mary Spencer. He d. Mar. 20, 1805. They had nine children, and one of them was named Solomon, who was b. in 1781, and d. in Madison, Conn. He m. Sally Richmond, who d. in 1840, in Bethany, N. Y., and they had ten children:

Solomon,
Sally,
Darius,
Roxanna,
Elisha,
Hannah,

Reuben,
Norris,
Solomon B.,
Samuel W. Dana.

Sally Cone, gt. gt. gr. dau. of Matthew Smith 4th, m. Alexander Leet and d. in Milan, Mich. They had seven children:
Eliza Ann,
Malvina,
George,
Menjo,
Martha,
Eliza Ann,
Harriet.

Eliza Ann and Harriet d. young and Martha m. a Mr. Marvin and resides in Milan, Mich.

Darius Cone, gt. gt. gr. son of Matthew Smith 4th, m. 1st, Betsey Parmelee. He d. at Canisteo, N. Y., and she d. in Ogden, N. Y. They had a daughter, Martha, who m. Derminic Le Valley, and resides in Hamilton, Ontario.

Roxanna Cone, gt. gt. gr. dau. of Matthew Smith 4th, m. Frederick Baird. She d. at Colorado City, Col., and he d. in Edford, Ill., Sept., 1861. They had eight children:

1. Mabel Maria, b. Feb. 18, 1819, and d. Aug. 20, 1850, in Alabama, N. Y.

2. Sarah Louisa, b. Feb., 1821, d. Aug., 1840, near Lockport. N. Y.

3. Gustavus J., b. Aug. 21 or 28, 1823, m. Lerusa M. Failing; they now reside in Alabama, N. Y., and have two children, Berton G., b. Feb. 27, 1868, and Helen P., b. Oct. 22, 1872.

4. Frederick N.

5. Solomon Truman, b. Feb., 1829, d. Aug., 1830.

6. Wm. J.

7. Hannah E., m. ——— Roe; writes her name Mrs. N. H. Roe and resides in Fort Scott, Kan.

8. Rosalthe L., m. A. T. Cone, who is dead. She resides in Colorado Springs, Col.

Elisha Cone, gt. gt. gr. son of Matthew 4th, b. Jan. 1, 1803, in Wallingford, Conn., m. Jan. 1, 1826, Eliza Ann Hill, who was b. April 18, 1810, in Bloomfield, N. Y., and resides in Orange City, Florida. He d. Sept. 6. 1846, at Geneseo, Ill. They had five children, as follows :

1. Harriet Thermuthis, b. Dec. 26, 1826, in Victor, N. Y., and m. Dec. 22, 1842, Wm. Miller. They now reside in Geneseo, Ill. Had children : (1) George Lewis, b. Dec. 2, 1843, in Geneseo, Ill., and d. Nov. 5, 1844 ; (2) Emily Effalina, b. Mar. 31, 1846, m. June 29, 1871, Rev. W. S. Read, and resides in Plymouth, Ill ; (3) George William, b. July 7, 1850, m. Nov. 10, 1885, Lydia Ann Goodwin, and resides in St. Joseph, Mo. He is freight auditor K. C., St. J. & C. B. R. R.

2. Clarissa Fidelia, b. June 28, 1830, in Stafford, N. Y., m. Mar. 9, 1848, Elisha M. Stewart. They reside in Latham, Kan., and had children : (1) James Watts, b. July 4, 1849, m. Julia Gaines ; served in the war—90 days call ; (2) Clara Eliza, m. J. F. Kinsey ; (3) William Josiah ; (4) Harriet Adelia ; (5) Charles Elisha ; (6) Jennie Frances.

3. Francis Solomon, b. Aug. 31, 1833, at Bergen, N. Y., m. May 15, 1855, Gabriella Gilmore, and has children : (1) Frank Gilmore, who resides in Chicago ; (2) Inez, b. Dec. 23, 1877, at Port Byron, Ill. Francis S. was in the 126th Ill. Reg., was Lieut. and Adjt., and now resides in Crescent City, Florida, engaged in orange culture.

4. Ellen Augusta, b. Jan. 18, 1836, at Bergen, N. Y., m. June 17, 1856, Roderick Manville, and had two children : (1) Arthur Henry, m. Mar. 3, 1881, Frances Emerson Watson. He is associate editor of the Jacksonville Times ; (2) Roderick Winfred, b. June 23, 1874, at Lake George, Florida, and d. Oct. 4, 1876.

5. Charles Elisha, b. Jan. 24, 1846, in Geneseo, Ill., and d. Mar. 29, 1863, in hospital at Nashville, Tenn. He was in the 8th Kansas Reg.

Hannah Cone, gt. gt. gr. dau. of Matthew Smith 4th, m. James Leet (of North Guilford, Conn.), an older brother of Alexander Leet, and had eight or more children, among them, James, Ursula, Mary and John.

Reuben Cone, gt. gt. gr. son of Matthew Smith 4th, was b. Mar. 3, 1807, d. Dec. 21, 1883.

Norris Cone, gt. gt. gr. son of Matthew Smith 4th, was b. Dec. 22, 1808, and d. Aug. 18, 1885.

Solomon B. Cone, gt. gt. gr. son of Matthew Smith 4th, m. 1st, Lucretia ———, and had children : Hiram, Sarah, William, Mary, etc. He resides with 2d wife in Hartwick, N. Y.

Samuel W. Dana Cone, gt. gt. gr. son of Matthew Smith 4th, d. Dec., 1853.

Ashbel Cone, son of Mary, gr. son of Matthew Smith 4th, was b. Aug. 2, 1747.

Jeremiah Cone, son of Mary, gr. son of Matthew Smith 4th, b. Feb. 7. 1750, m. 1st, Aug. 10, 1773, Mary Brockway ; and, 2d, July 25, 1776, Ruth Spencer.

Elizabeth Cone, dau. of Mary, gr. dau. of Matthew Smith 4th, was b. Aug. 22, 1751.

Theodore Cone, son of Mary, gr. son of Matthew Smith 4th, was b. Aug. 12, 1758.

V.

Lydia (5th child), dau. of Matthew Smith 4th, gr. dau. of Matthew 3d, b. Feb. 24, 1718, m. Feb. 24, 1743, Josiah Arnold, b. Mar. 24, 1715. She d. May 31, 1747, and was buried in the Cove burying ground in E. Haddam, Conn. They had three children.

CHILDREN :

I.—Lydia, b. Nov. 15, 1743. } Twins.
II.—Elizabeth, b. Nov. 15, 1743.
III.—Josiah, b. Aug. 29, 1745.

Descendants of Ruth Smith and Jared Cone.

—:o:—

VI.

Ruth. dau. of Matthew Smith 4th, gr. dau. of Matthew 3d, b. Mar. 29, 1720, m. Dec., 1738, Jared Cone (brother of Joseph Cone, who married Ruth's sister Mary), b. Jan 12, 1715, and d. Oct. 10, 1781. She d. Oct. 13, 1748.

CHILDREN:

I.—Matthew, b. Oct. 15, 1739, d. Dec. 15, 1739.
II.—Matthew, b. Oct. 14, 1740.
III.—Nehemiah, b. Sept. 14, 1742.
IV.—Ruth, b. July 28, 1745.
V.—Sarah, b. Mar. 19, 1748.

2. Matthew Cone, son of Ruth, gr. son of Matthew Smith 4th, b. Oct. 14, 1740, m. 1st, June 24, 1760, Mary Barnes, who d. April 27, 1768, and m. 2d, Sept. 13, 1770, Lydia Gates, having three children by first marriage and two by second marriage.

CHILDREN: (1st marriage.)

I.—Lucy, b. July 20, 1761.
II.—Zenas, b. Nov. 8, 1763.
III.—Newell, b. Aug. 28, 1765.

(2d marriage.)

IV.—Ephraim, b. Aug. 25, 1771.
V.—Jared, b. April 6, 1781.

Ephraim Cone, son of Matthew Cone, gr. son of Ruth, gt. gr. son of Matthew Smith 4th, b. Aug. 25, 1771, m., in 1798, Lucy Hart, who was b. in 1783 and d. Aug., 1855, in Attica, N. Y. They had three children:

Alonzo, b. 1799, d. in 1853.

Ephraim, b. June 1, 1805, m. Rachel P. Jenkins, and d. April 26, 1868,

Orville, b. Jan. 27, 1809.

Jared Cone, son of Matthew Cone, gr. son of Ruth, gt. gr. son of Matthew Smith 4th, b. April 6, 1781, m. 1st, Oct. 4, 1804, Hannah Beebe, who was b. Dec. 20, 1781, and d. Oct. 22, 1822. He m. 2d, Dec. 4, 1823, Elizabeth Shoft, who was b. July 5, 1794, and d. May, 1851. He d. Oct. 13, 1856. There were by 1st marriage seven children, and by 2d marriage, five children.

CHILDREN: (1st marriage.)

Jared, b. Aug. 23, 1805, d. June 13, 1885.
Lucy, b. Dec. 6, 1807, d. Nov. 18, 1870.
Edmond, b. Feb. 2, 1810, d. Feb. 22, 1884.
Stewart B., b. June 25, 1812, d. Aug. 4, 1885.
Margaret S., b. July 15, 1815, d. Dec., 1876.
Apollos, b. Dec. 12, 1817.
Huldah, b. Aug. 3, 1820, d. June 26, 1861.

(2d marriage.)

Barton, b. Aug. 23, 1824, d. Dec. 20, 1887.
Hawley, b. Jan. 11, 1826.
Hannah, b. May 3, 1828.
Philip, b. Feb. 11, 1833.
Newell, b. Feb. 27, 1836, d.

3. Nehemiah Cone, son of Ruth, gr. son of Matthew Smith 4th, b. Sept. 14, 1742, m. June 7, 1764, Jededidah Andrews. He d. Sept. 4, 1809.

CHILDREN:

I. Statyra, b. May 1, 1772, m. Dudley Gates.
II. Polly, b. July 10, 1774, d. May 21, 1858, unmarried.
III. Sarah, b. Oct. 8, 1777.
IV. Newell, b. Sept. 2, 1779, m. Oct. 4, 1802, Anna Silliman, who d. July 9, 1860. He d. April 19, 1856. They had five children.

CHILDREN:

Albert S., b. Jan. 3, 1804, d. April 10, 1873.
Wm. E., b. Sept. 24, 1805, d. Feb. 20, 1886.
Addison, b. Oct. 14, 1807, d. Jan. 21, 1884.
Aristarchus, b. Feb. 2, 1815.
Julius, b. April 9, 1817, d. July 6, 1822.

V. Jared, b. Dec. 21, 1781, m. Damaris Cone (dau. of Geo. Cone), who was b. July 11, 1781, and d. April 10, 1868. He d. Feb., 1847.

CHILDREN:

Philena, b. Dec. 21, 1807.
Norman, b. Sept. 30, 1810.
Francis, b. April 12, 1812, m. Laura Clark. He d. July 17, 1854.
Eliza, b. Mar. 7, 1814, m. 1st, Nathan Loomis, and 2d, Geo. Anderson. She resides in E. Hartford, Conn.
Marintha, b. Nov. 19, 1819, d. in 1879, m. Linus Atkins.
Daniel, b. May 8, 1823, d. in 1846.

VI. Betsey, b. 1784, d. Oct., 1860, unmarried.
VII. Lucy, b. 1785, d. Oct. 5, 1862, unmarried.

4. Ruth Cone, dau. of Ruth, gr. dau. of Matthew Smith 4th, b. July 28, 1745, m. Ashbel Olmstead.

5. Sarah, dau. of Ruth, gr. dau of Matthew Smith 4th, b. Mar. 19, 1748, m. Jeremiah Sibley.

VII.

Matthew Smith 5th, son of Matthew 4th, gr. son of Matthew 3d, b. Nov. 1, 1722, in E. Haddam, Conn., m. Jan. 16, 1745, Sarah Church, who was b. July 4, 1724, and d. July 21, 1796. He d. Oct. 9, 1804.

(For convenience, the 8th child of Matthew 4th is now inserted and the record will be *complete* from Matthew 5th, with the exception of one family, viz.: Elizabeth Smith and her descendants.)

VIII.

Susanna, dau. of Matthew 4th, gr. dau. of Matthew 3d, b. in 1725, m. in 1744, Nehemiah Tracy, who was b. in 1723. He d. Sept. 9, 1776, and she d. April 20, 1806; both buried in Mt. Parnassus graveyard at E. Haddam, Conn.

CHILDREN:

I.—Susanna, b. Mar. 14, 1745.
II.—Tryphena, b. June 9, 1746, d. young.
III.—Tryphena, b. April 14, 1748.
IV.—Jerusha, b. Oct. 23, 1751.
V.—Nehemiah, b. Nov. 8, 1753.
VI.—Sarah, b. June 15, 1755.
VII.—Rachel, b. Mar. 18, 1757.
VIII.—Gamaliel R., b. Feb. 17, 1759.
IX.—Hannah S., b. Oct. 20, 1760.
X.—Jedediah, b. Oct. 16, 1762.
XI.—Daniel, b. Jan. 9, 1765.
XII.—Elizabeth, b. July 5, 1767.
XIII.—Eliphalet, b. May 1, 1772.

The greater part of this family left East Haddam, Conn., early in life. Nehemiah, after living some years on the old homestead, removed to Smithfield, Pa., and is said to have given the place its name, and his descendants now live there.

Gamaliel and Daniel settled in Colchester, Conn.

Descendants of Matthew Smith 5th.

———:o:———

Matthew 5th, son of Matthew 4th, gr. son of Matthew 3d, b. in E. Haddam, Conn., Nov. 1, 1722, m. Jan. 16, 1745, Sarah Church, who was b. July 4, 1724, and d. July 21, 1796. He d. Oct. 9, 1804.

Dec. 10, 1792, he made his will and wrote a letter to his children, and the following is a copy of the same:

"IN THE NAME OF GOD, AMEN, I, Matthew Smith of East Haddam, Conn., in the county of Middlesex, enjoying usual health of body and soundness of mind, do make and ordain this, my last will and testament:

Item.—I give to my beloved wife Sarah one-third part of my movable estate and the use or improvement of one-third part of all my lands and buildings during her natural life.

Item.—I give to my son Matthew ninety pounds, my great Bible, a red chest, the first volume of Locke on Human Understanding, a large pair of tongs and one-third part of my wearing apparel.

Item.—I give to my son Calvin, above what he has already received, the second volume of Locke on Human Understanding, one-third part of my wearing apparel and thirty pounds, to be paid in stock or country produce.

Item.—I give to my daughter Elizabeth so much as will make the sum of fifty pounds, including what she has already received.

Item.—I give to my daughter Sarah fifty pounds, a loom and all the tackling, and the privilege of occupying the north room in my dwelling so long as she shall remain single, and the privilege of keeping one cow and ten sheep on my favour, from year to year, so long as she shall remain in single life.

Item.—I give to my son Jeremiah my dwelling house and barn and out-houses, and all my land, goods and chattels, including all my estate, both real and personal, subject to the encumbrance and legacies above named, and which shall remain after my debts and funeral charges shall be paid.

(3)

Finally, I do nominate and appoint my son Jeremiah executor of this my last will and testament.

In testimony whereof I do now set my hand and seal, this 10th day of December, 1792.

MATTHEW SMITH. [SEAL.]

Signed and sealed in presence of Israel Champion, Elijah Parsons, Francis Beckwith.

Dec. 10, 1792.—My dear children:

I have this day made my last will and testament. I have divided to you my estate, which it has pleased God to give me, in such proportions as, after long deliberation, I think just and right, without particular favor or partiality to any one I pray God that you may live in peace and that a divine blessing may attend you and yours to the latest posterity;—it is my advice and charge to you to avoid all contentions in regard to the several divisions and proportions I have assigned you, and I hope you will believe that I have acted according to my wisdom and without any bias or prejudice for or against any one.

I bid you farewell, and while I live I shall continue to pray that we may meet together in a better world and be heirs of the heavenly inheritance.

MATTHEW SMITH.

CHILDREN : (of Matthew 5th.)

I.—Asa, b. July 9, 1747.
II.—Elizabeth, b. Nov. 12, 1750.
III.—Matthew, b. May 12, 1753.
IV.—Azariah, b. May 16, 1755.
V.—Jeremiah, b. June 29, 1758.
VI.—Calvin, b. Nov. 28, 1760.
VII.—Sarah, b. Aug. 14, 1764.

Asa, son of Matthew 5th, gr. son of Matthew 4th, b. July 9, 1747, in E. Haddam, Conn., and d. Aug. 2, 1767. He was found dead near the residence of Wm. H. Ayres, where he went to attend a social gathering in the evening. He was not found until after a search of two days, and then only a short distance from the house. The cause of his death ever remained a mystery. He was buried in the Cove burying ground.

Descendants of Elizabeth Smith.

——:o:——

Elizabeth, dau. of Matthew 5th, gr. dau. of Matthew 4th, b. Nov. 12, 1750, in E. Haddam, Conn., m. Oliver Ackley, who was b. in 1750 and d. Sept. 17, 1827. She d. April 4, 1815, and both were buried at Rock Landing, E. Haddam, Conn. He kept a hotel and was a blacksmith. But little can be ascertained of this family, probably because of their early departure to Ohio.

From the Middle Haddam church records we learn that Oliver Ackley was son of Benjamin Ackley, and that he was baptized Dec. 2, 1750, and that his wife, Elizabeth Ackley,' united with the church there Sept. 2, 1781, and also that three of their children were baptized Dec. 2, 1781, one Sept. 9, 1787, and one Nov. 8, 1789. It is known that they had six children:

1. Rebecca.
2. Polly.
3. Elizabeth.
4. Asa, who m. (it is thought a person named Young), worked with his father, blacksmithing, and built and ironed off an ox wagon, with hoop bows overhead, with which to emigrate to Ohio. He had children, among them a boy who was a ringleader among the boys.
5. Sally.
6. Oliver, who m. Feb. 6, 1808, Susan Strong. Oliver Ackley, Senior, married, after the death of his wife, Matilda Cole, who had been his housekeeper.

With the exception of the record of the descendants of the above family, the genealogy will now be found to be complete except in a few instances, where letters have been repeatedly sent and the parties have neglected or not desired to answer.

Descendants of Matthew 6th.

———: o :———

Matthew 6th, son of Matthew 5th, gr. son of Matthew 4th, b. May 12, 1753, at E. Haddam, Conn., m. 1st, Dec., 1777, Asenath Anable, who was b. Feb. 4, 1756. She d. Dec. 14, 1825, in Middlefield, Mass. He m. 2d, July 30, 1826, Mrs. Elizabeth Gates (*née* Percival), who was b. July 19, 1755, and d. Nov. 23, 1835. He d. July 30, 1833, in Middlefield, Mass. He was a leading man in the affairs of the town, known and respected in all the region about as a man of superior character and capacity. He served a term in the State Legislature, and for many years held commissions from the governor as justice of the peace and captain of the militia. He moved to Middlefield, Mass., about 1783.

CHILDREN:

(All by 1st marriage.)

I.—Anna, b. June, 1778.
II.—Azariah, b. June, 1780.
III.—Anna, b. July 30, 1782.
IV.—Azariah, b. Dec. 7, 1784.
V.—Matthew, b. Aug. 25, 1787.
VI.—Joseph, b. Sept. 28, 1789.
VII.—John, b. Sept. 29, 1792, d. Sept. 10, 1811.
VIII.—Asenath, b. Oct. 21, 1794, d. Sept. 27, 1810.
IX.—Samuel, b. Aug. 28, 1797.

I.

Anna, dau. of Matthew 6th, gr. dau. of Matthew 5th, b. June, 1778, in E. Haddam, Conn., and d. there, July 7, 1782, and was buried in Mt. Parnassus graveyard.

II.

Azariah, son of Matthew 6th, gr. son of Matthew 5th, b. June, 1780, in E. Haddam, Conn., and d. there, July 22, 1782, and was buried in Mt. Parnassus graveyard.

Descendants of Anna Smith.

——:o:——

III.

Anna, dau. of Matthew 6th, gr. dau. of Matthew 5th, b. July 30, 1782, in E. Haddam, Conn., m. 1st, June 19, 1806, Clark Martin, who was b. Dec. 31, 1779, in Washington, Mass., and was drowned there, July 12, 1823, and buried there. She m. 2d, June 26, 1826, Daniel Root, who was b. Jan. 4, 1769, in Enfield, Conn., and d. Oct. 7, 1850, in Middlefield, Mass. She d. July 10, 1859, at the home of her oldest daughter, in Portage, Wisconsin. She was a woman of rare solidity of character, of great practical common sense and exceptional intelligence.

CHILDREN: (1st marriage.)

I.—Anna, b. Mar. 23, 1807.
II.—Asenath Smith, b. May 13, 1810.
III.—John Clark, b. May 9, 1814.
IV.—Thomas, b. Aug. 29, 1818.

1. Anna Martin, dau. of Anna, gr. dau. of Matthew 6th, b. Mar. 23, 1807, in Washington, Mass., m. June 25, 1828, Elisha Andrew Wells, who was b. in Hartford, Conn., Sept. 9, 1801, and d. at Portage, Wisconsin, June 26, 1885. She resided with her daughter at Van Wert, Ohio, and d. May 3, 1890.

CHILDREN:

I.—Ann Clarissa, b. Nov. 29, 1829.
II.—Caroline Asenath, b. Dec. 28, 1831, d. Mar. 3, 1849.
III.—Martha Eliza, b. Jan. 9, 1834.
IV.—Horace Elisha, b. June 7, 1836.
V.—Lydia Viola, b. Dec. 3, 1838.
VI.—Lemuel Martin, b. Mar. 25, 1842.
VII.—Jane Celine, b. July 16, 1844, d. Sept. 9, 1845.
VIII.—Henry Clark, b. May 4, 1845, d. Aug. 16, 1845.
IX.—Mary Alice, b. Feb. 3, 1853.

Ann Clarissa Wells, dau. of Anna, gr. dau. of Anna, b. Nov. 29, 1829, m. July 19, 1863, Hugh McFarlane, who was b. at Plumb Bridge, County Tyrone, Tyrone, Ireland, June 22, 1815. He came to this country when nineteen years of age, and first located at Mineral Point, Wisconsin, for nine years, then went to Columbia county, to Arlington. Was assemblyman two or three times; was a farmer; nearest P. O. was Poynette. He d. Aug. 16, 1882, and she d. with a malignant cancer, Oct. 10, 1884.

CHILDREN:

I.—Clara Wells, b. Sept. 18, 1864.
II.—Hugh, b. June 26, 1867.

Clara W. McFarlane, dau. of Ann Clarissa, gr. dau. of Anna, b. Sept. 18, 1864, m. Sept. 18, 1885, Ernest Gerstenkorn, who was b. April 23, 1862, in Milwaukee, Wis. He is a R. R. engineer.

CHILDREN:

I.—Laura Bertha, b. Dec. 24, 1885.

Caroline Asenath Wells, dau. of Anna, gr. dau. of Anna, b. Dec. 28, 1831, and d. Mar. 3, 1849.

Martha Eliza Wells, dau. of Anna, gr. dau. of Anna, b. Jan. 9, 1834, m. Oct. 30, 1855, Caleb Strong Crossman, who was b. April 14, 1814, in Boylston, Mass, and d. Aug. 31, 1889, at his home, Van Wert, Ohio, where he had resided twenty-two years. All his life he was a student and teacher of music. In his career as a musician it was his lot to be one of the anvil chorus in the "Peace Jubilee," held in Boston shortly after the close of the civil war. Prof. Crossman was buried at Shirley Village, Mass. No children.

Horace Elisha Wells, son of Anna, gr. son of Anna, b. June 7, 1836, m. Sept. 15, 1862, Julia W. Weston, who was b. Aug. 15, 1836. He resided for some time at Elyria, Ohio, being in business in Cleveland, Ohio. In 1889, he was president of the Advance News Co., in Chicago, Ill.

CHILDREN:

I.—Alice Maud, b. Dec. 8, 1864, d. Sept. 15, 1865.

Lydia Viola Wells, dau. of Anna, gr. dau. of Anna, b. Dec. 3, 1838, m. May 6, 1863, Charles Randall Gallett, who was b. Jan. 6, 1833, in Benton Center, N. Y. They reside in Portage, Wisconsin.

CHILDREN:

I.—Sarah, b. April 10, 1864. She graduated at the University of Wisconsin in 1886, with the degree of A. B.
II.—Henry Wells, b. Feb. 14, 1866.
III.—Anna, b. Dec. 5, 1869, d. Mar. 9, 1889.
IV.—Robt. Mitchell, b. July 31, 1875.
V.—Charles Horace, b. Mar. 21, 1878, d. Nov. 30, 1882.
VI.—James Randall, b. Feb. 24, 1881.
VII.—Harriet Mary, b. Aug. 11, 1883.

Lemuel Martin Wells, son of Anna, gr. son of Anna, b. Mar. 25, 1842, m. Mar. 7, 1864, Maria L. Cobb, who was b. June 17, 1845. She now resides at Cedar Falls, Iowa.

CHILDREN:

I.—Horace Leonard, b. Feb. 16, 1865.
II.—Anna, b. Aug. 11, 1866.
III.—Blanche, b. Jan. 10, 1868.

Horace Leonard Wells, son of Lemuel M., gr. son of Anna, b. Feb. 16, 1865, m. Sept. 23, 1888, Mary Cole, who was b. Aug. 10, 1866, in Forest City, Iowa.

CHILDREN:

I.—Leila A., b. May 7, 1890.

Jane Celine Wells, dau. of Anna, gr. dau. of Anna, b. July 16, 1844, and d. Sept. 9, 1845.

Henry Clark Wells, son of Anna, gr. son of Anna, b. May 4, 1845, and d. Aug. 16, 1845.

Mary Alice Wells, dau. of Anna, gr. dau. of Anna, b. Feb. 3, 1853, and in 1890 was unmarried and resided at Van Wert, Ohio, until the death of her mother, when she went to Portage, Wis. She is now in Chicago, with her brother Horace.

2. Asenath Smith Martin, dau. of Anna, gr. dau. of Matthew 6th, b. May 13, 1810, in Washington, Mass., m. April 2, 1832, James Noble, who was b. Nov. 23, 1809, in Washington, Mass., and removed to Hartford, Conn., about 1829, where he has been in business, grocery, clothing, and in 1890 was engaged in market gardening, running a store in connection with the same. She d. Sept. 29, 1837.

CHILDREN:

1.—James Martin, b. Nov. 30, 1834.
II.—Asenath, b. Sept 18, 1837.

James Martin Noble, son of Asenath, gr. son of Anna, b. Nov. 30, 1834, in Hartford, Conn., m. April 24, 1862, Mary Brewer, who was b. Aug. 13, 1842, in Manchester, Conn., and in 1890 resided in Hartford, Conn.

CHILDREN:

I.—William B., b. Feb. 18, 1863.
II.—Thomas Martin, b. Feb. 21, 1866.
III.—Charles Spencer, b. Oct. 30, 1873.

William Brewer Noble, son of James Martin, gr. son of Asenath, b. Feb. 18, 1863, in Hartford, Conn., m. Nov. 9, 1887, Nettie B. Sherman, who was b. Oct. 7, 1866. In 1890, resided in E. Hartford, Conn. He is a druggist.

CHILDREN:

I.—Harry Sherman, b. April 30, 1888, d. June 29, 1889.

Thomas Martin Noble, son of James M., gr. son of Asenath, b. Feb. 21, 1866, in E. Hartford, Conn., and in 1890 resided in Hartford, Conn.

Charles Spencer Noble, son of James Martin, gr. son of Asenath, b. Oct. 30, 1873, in East Hartford, Conn., and in 1890 resided in Hartford, Conn.

Asenath Noble, dau. of Asenath, gr. dau. of Anna, b. Sept. 18, 1837, in Hartford, Conn., m. Oct. 14, 1858, Edwin Luce Humphrey, who was b. July 31, 1835, in Pittsfield, Mass. He is engaged in burning lime and in quarrying stone, in Pittsfield, Mass.

CHILDREN: (all born in Pittsfield, Mass.)

I.—Charles Edwin, b. Aug. 5, 1859.
II.—Ida Norma, b. May 30, 1861.

(4)

III.—Edward Yates, b. Dec. 30, 1863.
IV.—Susan Asenath, b. Feb. 27, 1870.
V.—Albert Noble, b. Dec. 12, 1872.

Charles Edwin Humphrey, son of Asenath, gr. son of Asenath, b. Aug. 5, 1859, in Pittsfield, Mass., and in 1890 was a commercial traveler.

Ida Norma, dau. of Asenath, gr. dau. of Asenath, b. May 30, 1861, in Pittsfield, Mass., m. April 12, 1881, Clinton Edgar Woods, who was b. Feb. 7, 1863, in Belchertown, Mass., and in 1890, was working for an electric light company, in Pittsburgh, Pa.

CHILDREN:

I.—Florence Estella, b. Dec. 12, 1882.

Edward Yates Humphrey, son of Asenath, gr. son of Asenath, b. Dec. 30, 1863, in Pittsfield, Mass, and in 1890 was a commercial traveler.

Susan Asenath Humphrey, dau. of Asenath, gr. dau. of Asenath, b. Feb. 27, 1870, in Pittsfield, Mass., and, in 1890, unmarried, and living in Pittsfield, Mass.

Albert Noble Humphrey, son of Asenath, gr. son of Asenath b. Dec. 12, 1872, in Pittsfield, Mass., and in 1890 resided there.

3. John Clark Martin, son of Anna, gr. son of Matthew 6th b. May 9, 1814, in Washington, Mass., m. April 30, 1837, Maria

Louisa Harper, who was b. Jan. 1, 1815, in Harpersfield, Ohio. His father died when he was nine years old, and when he was ten his mother offered him the present of a nice book, if he would cultivate a piece of land and raise potatoes, and do it well, and as a result of his labors he carried into the cellar thirty bushels, and received " Robin Hood," with which he was then very much delighted. Soon after he went to Middlefield, Mass., to work for his uncle Samuel until he was twenty-one, going to school winters and receiving a good education, and teaching school some. Soon after he went to Ohio, married and settled in Russell, then moved to Locke, Michigan (P. O. address being Williamston), where he has preached, as opportunity offered, and is a farmer. They have no children but an adopted son, who is married and lives near them, to care for them in their declining years.

4. Thomas Martin, son of Anna, gr. son of Matthew 6th, b. Aug. 29, 1818, in Washington, Mass., m. 1st, April 16, 1843, Permelia Wheat, who was b. April 22, 1820, in Glastonbury, Conn., and d. Jan. 1, 1887, in Hartford, Conn., having been for thirty years an invalid and a great sufferer much of the time for the last twenty years.

He m. 2d, Nov. 1, 1887, Sophia Smith (dau. of John, gr. dau. of Matthew 7th, who was b. April 21, 1847, in Middlefield, Mass., and is the author of "Mack Genealogy" and of this work, also). At the age of seventeen he went to Hartford, Conn., having previously been there during the winter of 1834–35, attending the Grammar school, and since then has made his home there. For the first ten years he was in the employ of his brother-in-law, James Noble, who was a manufacturer of and wholesale and retail dealer in, ready-made clothing.

In 1848 he began business on his own account, in the retail grocery trade, which, under his tact and active business qualities, soon grew to large proportions, so that in 1850 the sales amounted to one hundred and twenty thousand dollars. After 1850 he added to the business a candle factory, and the sales were large, and not only embraced the New England States, but New York and even Michigan. In those days the use of tallow candles was not despised even in the best families, and the business was large and the profits considerable. (His integrity in business was never tarnished, thus his credit was never questioned.) He continued in that business until 1857, when he dropped it and took up the buying of hides and fat, curing the hides and trying the fat. This, too, soon grew to large proportions and was prosecuted with energy until the close of the War of the Rebellion, when, finding the business could be closed up and leave him with a fair competence, he concluded to let others do the business, while he retired and looked after his investments, the principal of which was stock in the Hartford Bridge Co., until 1889, when the bridge became free. The company wound up its affairs early in 1890. In 1865 he became director, then president, and since 1877 has been secretary and treasurer. In the "Hartford Times," dated Nov. 20, 1889, is found the following: " Mr. Thomas Martin was identified with the bridge company for fifty-five years. In 1834 he was employed to fill and light the lamps. He filled the lamps in the morning, saturating the wicks with spirits of turpentine. In the early evening he went through the bridge with a torch and lighted them; this, seven days in the week, for which he received fifty cents! or seven cents, one mill and three-sevenths of a mill *per day*. Think of that, poor young man of 1889. He worked his way, attending the old Grammar School on Linden Place, and earning money enough to support himself in the odd hours of the school's recesses," etc. His deeds of charity are many, but given in a quiet way.

CHILDREN: (1st marriage.)

I.—Anna Permelia, b. Sept. 19, 1848, d. Sept. 13, 1859.

Descendants of Azariah Smith.

——:o:——

IV.

Azariah, son of Matthew 6th, gr. son of Matthew 5th, b. Dec. 7, 1784, in Middlefield, Mass., m. Aug. 29, 1811, Zilpah Mack, who was b. Feb. 3, 1788, in Middlefield, Mass., and d. Mar. 14, 1871, in Manlius, N. Y. He was brought up on his father's farm, where he lived until 1807. His early education was acquired in the common schools, supplemented by one winter's attendance at the academy at Westfield, Mass.

In 1807 he went to Manlius, N. Y., where he engaged in mercantile business, which, with cotton manufacturing, was his employment through life. He was widely known as a man of remarkable business capacity, generosity, public spirit and perfect integrity, and was often selected for important trusts.

In 1824 he was a presidential elector, and as such voted for John Quincy Adams.

In 1838, 1839 and 1840 he was a member of Assembly for Onondaga Co., N. Y.

That he was an active supporter of the cause of education is shown by the noteworthy fact that at the time of his decease he was a trustee of the common school district where he resided, of Manlius Academy, of Hamilton College and of Auburn Theological Seminary; being, at the same time, trustee of one institution in each grade of the educational system of New York.

He resided at Manlius until his death, which occurred Nov. 12, 1846, at New Haven, Conn., where he had gone in hopes of benefiting his health.

CHILDREN: (all born in Manlius, N. Y.)

I.—Calvin, b. April 17, 1812, d. Nov. 9, 1812, at Manlius, N. Y.

II.—John Calvin, b. Sept. 14, 1813.

III.—Azariah, b. Sept. 19, 1815, d. Sept. 13, 1816, at Manlius, N. Y.
    IV.—Azariah, b. Feb. 16, 1817.
    V.—Charles, b. July 13, 1818.
    VI.—Mary, b. July 21, 1820, d. Aug. 1, 1821, at Manlius, N. Y.
    VII.—William Manlius, b. Sept. 26, 1823.
    VIII.—Zilpha, b. April 1, 1825.

2. John Calvin Smith, son of Azariah, gr. son of Matthew 6th, b. Sept. 14, 1813, in Manlius, N. Y., m. June 2, 1835, Catharine Eliza Storm, who was b. Nov. 15, 1814, at New York City. He received an academic education and was brought up a merchant. He kept store at Manlius, N. Y., nine years, and was in the wholesale trade in New York City, twenty-one years.

In 1865 he retired from business, and since then resided at Manlius, N. Y., until his death, Aug. 21, 1883.

CHILDREN:

I.—Louisa, b. June 3, 1836.

Louisa Smith, dau. of John Calvin, gr. dau. of Azariah, b. June 3, 1836, m. Sept. 16, 1857, Peter Van Shaack, who was b. April 7, 1832, in Manlius, N. Y. She was educated at Mrs. Cooke's school in Bloomfield, N. J., and Prof. H. B. Tappan's school in New York City. After her marriage she resided four years at Charleston, S. C., and since then has resided at Chicago, Ill., where her husband is a wholesale druggist.

CHILDREN:

    I.—John Calvin, b. July 2, 1858, in Manlius, N. Y.
    II.—Henry Cruger, b. Dec. 14, 1860, in Charleston, S. C.
    III.—Robert Hubbard, b. Mar. 21, 1862, in Mill Point, Ont.
    IV.—Cornelius Peter, } b. May 26, 1863, in Manlius, N. Y.
    V.—Catharine Louisa, }

John Calvin Van Schaack, son of Louisa, gr. son of John Calvin Smith, b. July 2, 1858, in Manlius, N. Y., m. Mar. 26, 1888, Florence Lilian Palmer, who was b. July 28, 1868, in Cincinnati, O. They have one child.

CHILDREN:

Calvin, b. April 1, 1889.

Henry Cruger Van Schaack, son of Louisa, gr. son of John Calvin Smith, b. Dec. 14, 1860, in Charleston, S. C., m. May 12, 1886, Renetta Sweet, who was b. Jan. 29, 1865, in Chicago, Ill. He is attorney-at-law and mortgage banker in Chicago, Ill.

CHILDREN:

Henry Cruger, b. Mar. 12, 1887.
Robert Cornelius, b. Oct. 1, 1888.

Robert Hubbard Van Schaack, son of Louisa, gr. son of John Calvin Smith, b. Mar. 21, 1862, at Mill Point, Ont., m. Nov. 2, 1887, Carrie Libby, who was b. Feb. 16, 1862, in Chicago, Ill. He is a member of the firm of Peter Van Schaack & Sons, wholesale druggists, Chicago, Ill.

CHILDREN:

Albione Libby, b. Sept. 18, 1888.
Robert Hubbard, b. Feb. 16, 1890.

Cornelius Peter Van Schaack, son of Louisa, gr. son of John Calvin Smith, b. May 26, 1863, in Manlius, N. Y., unmarried, and is a member of the firm of Peter Van Schaack & Sons, wholesale druggists, Chicago, Ill.

Catherine Louisa Van Schaack, dau. of Louisa, gr. dau. of John Calvin Smith, b. May 26, 1863, in Manlius, N. Y., and d. Sept. 12, 1885. She m. Dec. 27, 1882, Joseph Rathborne, who was b. Dec. 12, 1845, in Virginia, Ireland. He is a wholesale lumber dealer in Chicago, Ill. They had one child.

CHILDREN:

Joseph Cornelius, b. July 20, 1884.

4. Azariah Smith, son of Azariah, gr. son of Matthew 6th, b. Feb. 16, 1817, in Manlius, N. Y., m. July 6, 1848, Corinth S. Elder, who was b. Jan. 24, 1820, in Cortlandville, N. Y. He was a graduate of Yale College, Yale Medical Institute, New Haven Theological Seminary, and attended a course of lectures at the law school.

He was ordained Aug. 30, 1842, at Manlius, N. Y., as an evangelist, to labor in foreign fields; sailed from Boston as a missionary of the A. B. C. F. M., for Smyrna, Nov. 10, 1842, expecting to join Dr. Grant at Mosul, and engage with him and others in labors for the Mt. Nestorians. Disturbances in the country prevented his obtaining a passport, and the accomplishment of his plans was delayed until 1844. He reached Mosul but a short time previous to Dr. Grant's death. Finding the Nestorians greatly diminished and scattered by the war, it was thought wise to disband the mission, and he returned to the sea-coast. (It was on this journey that Dr. Smith first learned that there were a few men inquiring after the Truth, living in the city of Aintab, Syria). Having reached the sea-coast, he soon connected himself with the Armenian Turkish mission. His medical skill called him from place to place, and it was not until the fall of 1845 that he became a resident of Erzeroom, in Asia Minor, and he labored till July, 1847.

In 1846, while absent, his house was mobbed by the Armenians, because of his having received into his house an Armenian priest who was inquiring after the Truth; but God overruled it for good.

In the fall of 1847 he was commissioned to labor in Aintab, Syria. He reached the city in December, having been delayed by an attack of cholera while journeying. He found the light flickering and apparently just ready to go out, but the Lord had a great and glorious work in store for him. His legal, medical and biblical knowledge were brought into requisition, and from early morn till late at night, body, soul and mind were found " diligent in business, fervent in spirit, serving the Lord," till June 3, 1851, when, after a short but painful illness, the Lord called him to enter into his rest.

His wife, Corinth S. (Elder) Smith, continued for two more years to labor with the women, going from house to house, when a severe sickness compelled her return to this country, in the hope of restoration and return. She, however, did not so far regain strength as to make it prudent for her to resume her missionary work, and so she cheerfully devoted herself to a life of Christian usefulness and service in this country. Her home was chiefly with her brother-in-law (Rev. A. K. Strong, D. D.), where she lightened the domestic cares of the pastor's wife and actively engaged in all good works among the members of his congregation. She lived mainly for others, and died at the residence of Rev. Addison K. Strong, Sept. 8, 1888. She gently breathed her life away after a lingering illness, of which the later symptoms were chiefly debility and slowly progressive paralysis.

CHILDREN: (all born in Aintab, Syria.)

I.—Zilpha Abigail, b. Sept. 29, 1850, d. Oct. 7, 1850, in Aintab.

II.—Azariah, b. Feb. 19, 1852, d. Feb. 19, 1852, in Aintab.

5. Charles Smith, son of Azariah, gr. son of Matthew 6th, b. July 13, 1818, in Manlius, N. Y., m. Dec. 27, 1843, Julia Maria Huntington, who was b. Sept. 1, 1820. He was brought

up a merchant, commenced business at Manlius in 1843, and continued it there until his death, which was caused by a fall while visiting the glen at Watkins, N. Y. This was Aug. 7, 1855. In 1890 his widow resided with her daughter at Binghamton, N. Y.

CHILDREN: (all born in Manlius, N. Y.)

I.—Infant daughter, d. Sept. 1, 1844, in Manlius, N. Y.
II.—Julia Sophia, b. Aug. 2, 1845, d. Feb. 1, 1847, in Manlius, N. Y.
III.—Julia Sophia, b. Aug. 18, 1847.
IV.—Herbert Huntington, b. Jan. 22, 1851.
V.—Anna Louisa, b. April 15, 1853, d. May 6, 1854, at Manlius, N. Y.

Julia Sophia Smith, dau. of Charles, gr. dau. of Azariah, b. Aug. 18, 1847, in Manlius, N. Y., m. Nov. 4, 1875, John Manier, who was b. May 19, 1851. She graduated at Mount Holyoke Seminary. In 1890 they resided at Binghamton, N. Y. No children.

Herbert Huntington Smith, son of Charles, gr. son of Azariah, b. Jan. 22, 1851, in Manlius, N. Y., m. Oct. 5, 1878, Daisy W. Smith, who was b. Jan. 10, 1858, in Woburn, Mass. He attended Manlius Academy, and in 1868-70 took a special course at Cornell University, and, in 1870, accompanied Prof. C. F. Hartt to Brazil as his assistant in scientific work. Since then he has made four trips there, principally with the object of studying and collecting animals; from 1873-77 worked most of the time on the Amazon—later, at Rio de Janeiro, in 1878, he made two trips in the interest of the (then) Scribner's Monthly, and from 1881-86, accompanied by his wife and two assistants, made an extensive tour of exploration, especially of the Amazon river, following it in canoes to its sources, Mrs. Smith being the first white woman who ever saw the upper waters of the Amazon.

In 1888, he traveled in Mexico, and is now engaged in scientific work in the West Indies, under the auspices of the Royal Society and British Association. He has written in English, "Brazil, the Amazons and the Coast," and various magazine articles for "Scribner's," "The American Naturalist," etc.; and in Portuguese, "*De Rio de Janeiro a Cuyaba*," a publication of articles for the "Gazeta de Noticias," a Rio de Janeiro paper. At various times he has been employed in geological surveys of New York and Ohio and of Brazil. He did much of the work on entomological terms for the Century Encyclopædia (now in course of publication). He is a member of the American Geographical Society and also of the Geographical societies of Rio de Janeiro and Lisbon.

His wife is daughter of Daniel Smith, a well-known engraver of New York and Boston, and her grandfather on her mother's side was Rev. Wm. B. Tappan, the author of some of our well-known hymns.

They have one child, b. Nov. 5, 1886.

Holland Huntington ———

7. Wm. Manlius Smith, son of Azariah, gr. son of Matthew 6th, b. Sept. 26, 1823, in Manlius, N. Y., m. Aug. 6, 1847, Frances Louisa Hall, who was b. Mar. 25, 1826, in Durham, Conn. She was a teacher in a female seminary at Alton, Ill., and on her way home from there stopped at Manlius, N. Y., to visit him and his parents. His mother had invited to a family tea quite a number of relatives, and then the marriage took place, much to the surprise of all present. Wm. Manlius began attending the district school when three years old, and, being favored all his school life with good teachers and out of school hours his studies receiving considerable attention from his parents, he grew up with a love for books and a taste for reading. His father had a custom of giving to each of his children

a new copy of the Bible on the completion of its first reading through by course, and he received his before he was seven years old. He attended two or three select schools, studying in them Higher English, Latin and Greek, and in his tenth year was reading Virgil, but was not thoroughly drilled in these studies until he attended Manlius Academy, where he had most competent and thorough instruction in the grammar of these languages under the teaching of two Amherst graduates, W. H. Tyler and C. C. Bayley. His academic instruction was supplemented, especially in mathematics, by his father's oversight and direction. One summer in particular, he arranged for him to study his algebra from five o'clock in the morning till breakfast time, at six, his father sitting by, reading, but ready to explain anything hard of comprehension.

He was a pupil in Manlius Academy from its commencement, in 1835, till the end of the summer term of 1840, and the fall of that year entered as Freshman at Yale College, New Haven, Conn., graduating in the class of 1844. The first two years he roomed with his brother Azariah, who was there pursuing his theological studies. He says of him: "I have never before or since known a person whose whole life, even to minute details, was so thoroughly pervaded with the Christian spirit as was his, and in all the two years of this intimate association with him I never knew him to do a sinful act. A portion of his time not occupied with theological studies, he gave to furtherance of his medical knowledge by attending private courses of lectures given by Dr. William Tully, in Materia Medica, Chemistry and the Theory and Practice of Medicine. In one hour of social intercourse he frequently gave me abstracts of these lectures, and thus gave my mind a direction toward the pursuit of medical studies."

The winter of 1844 he spent in the office of Dr. Alden March, at Albany, and attended lectures at the Medical College there. In the summer of 1845, he took private instructions in medicine of Dr. William Tully, and in the winter attended the Medical College at Albany, and in the summer of 1846 returned to New Haven to be with Dr. Tully; also in 1847. In October, 1848, he began attendance on a full course of medical lectures at the

University of Pennsylvania, in Philadelphia, and received from that institution the degree of M. D., March, 1849. In June he opened an office in Syracuse, N. Y., and lived there till the fall of 1851, when it seemed desirable that he should return to Manlius to live with and care for his mother, and there he engaged in the practice of medicine till the fall of 1872 (with an intermission of 1857 and 1858), when he received an appointment to lecture on pharmacy, during the winter, in the New York College of Pharmacy.

In October, 1873, he established himself in chemical business in Syracuse, N. Y. From May, 1874, till December, 1875, was physician at the State prison at Sing Sing, N. Y., when he resigned and returned to his business at Syracuse. In 1877 he was made Professor of Materia Medica in the Syracuse University, and in 1878 exchanged places with the Professor of Chemistry, which position he still holds as well as Professor of Botany.

From the fact that he is a renowned chemist he has many times been consulted in cases of death from supposed poisoning, and made several examinations, in which he has been happily instrumental in demonstrating the innocence of the suspected party, and in a few cases where poison was found, for some reason the parties were not brought to trial.

He was in Utica a year and a half, acting as chemist in refining gold for a manufacturer of what was then known as sponge gold.

In Manlius he held the office of village trustee, and also of the schools, and of Manlius Academy, and was largely influential in having an academic department in the Union school at Manlius, and of turning over to its uses the property of the defunct academy. He was secretary of the Medical Society of Onondaga county for several years and of the Medical Society of the State of New York from 1877 to 1889; also secretary of the Manlius and Pompey Agricultural Association for upwards of twenty years.

He united with the College church in New Haven in 1841, and transferred his connection from that to the First Presbyterian church in Syracuse in 1849. When he returned to Manlius he became connected with its Presbyterian church and served many years as one of its trustees and its clerk and treasurer. A part of the time he was S. S. superintendent, and a few years before his last removal to Syracuse (in 1881), he was one of its elders.

He has for years suffered from malarial troubles, and his achievements have been less than they might otherwise have been. They have a large family and reside on Holland street, Syracuse, N. Y.

CHILDREN:

I.—Dullas, b. May 17, 1848, d. Sept. 20, 1849.
II.—Mary, b. Oct 31, 1850, d. Mar. 7, 1859.
III.—Zilpha, b. Aug 4, 1852.
IV.—Harriet, b. Nov. 4, 1854.
V.—Azariah, b. Aug. 7, 1856.
VI.—Aulus, b. July 18, 1858.
VII.—Walter (Storm), b. Feb. 7, 1860.
VIII.—Newton, b. Aug. 21, 1862.
IX.—Allen (Macy), b. June 26, 1864.
X.—Clara, b. Feb. 5, 1866.
XI.—Louisa, b. July 18, 1868.
XII.—Ludlow, b. Aug. 7, 1870.

I. Dullas Smith, son of Wm. Manlius, gr. son of Azariah, b. May 17, 1848, at Manlius, N. Y., and d. Sept. 20, 1849, at Syracuse, N. Y.

II. Mary Smith, dau. of Wm. Manlius, gr. dau. of Azariah, b. Oct. 31, 1850, at Syracuse, N. Y., and d. Mar. 7, 1859, at Manlius, N. Y.

III. Zilpha Smith, dau. of Wm. Manlius, gr. dau. of Azariah, b. Aug. 4, 1852, in Manlius, N. Y., m. Jan. 7, 1875, Lewis S. Tripp, who was b. Nov. 9, 1852, and d. July 14, 1875, in Manlius, N. Y. She was educated in the public schools at Manlius, N. Y., including the academy. She also attended the female seminary at Hamilton, N. Y. Since the death of her husband she has assisted her mother in the care of the household. She has one daughter:

Hattie Louise, b. Oct. 23, 1875, at Manlius, N. Y.

IV. Harriet Smith, dau. of Wm. Manlius, gr. dau. of Azariah, b. Nov. 4, 1854, in Manlius, N. Y., attended the schools in Manlius, with her sister, and at the age of eighteen took charge of the telegraph office at Palmyra, N. Y., and has been in the employ of the N. Y. C. R. R. Co. ever since. In 1873 and 1874 she was operator at Palmyra, Waterloo and Suspension Bridge, and in February, 1875, was sent to Holly, N. Y., and in June was put in charge of ticket office there. She remained at Holly until April, 1880, when she was transferred to Albion to assume a similar position. The Holly Standard has the following complimentary notice: "Miss Hattie Smith, who has for some years been the ticket agent and operator at the Holly depot, went to Albion on Tuesday to assume a similar position there, but at quite an advance in wages. We have heard and witnessed, within the last thirty-six hours, a great deal of sorrow and mourning over this change. Miss Smith has greatly endeared herself to the people of Holly, both in a business and social way. Everybody of course is glad to learn of her promotion and advance in a pecuniary sense, and their best wishes for her future success and happiness surely go with her."

She served in Albion, N. Y., until February, 1884, when she was transferred to Lockport, N. Y. The Albion Chronicle of Feb. 23, 1884, contained the following: "Miss Hattie Smith, who has been the Central-Hudson ticket agent at this station for four years past, has been transferred to Lockport to take charge of the ticket office in that city. Miss Smith, during her stay among us, has won a host of friends by her ladylike deportment and accommodating and courteous demeanor toward everyone. She left for her new field of labor Wednesday afternoon. The change was made on short notice, but a few of her friends near the depot clubbed together and procured a copy of Webster's Unabridged Dictionary, which, together with a standard, was forwarded to her the same evening." She remained at Lockport until December, 1886, when, at her own request, she was allowed to give up the tickets entirely, and was moved to the telegraph office in Syracuse, where she still remains.

V. Azariah Smith, son of Wm. Manlius, gr. son of Azariah, b. Aug. 7, 1856, in Manlius, N. Y., m. May 10, 1883, Edith K. Carter, who was b. Feb. 10, 1858, in London, Eng. He d. Feb. 23, 1887, leaving one child, Gurdon Bradley, b. Jan. 28, 1885. His widow and child now reside in Providence, R. I. He had learned the trade of a machinist, and at the time of his death was in the employ of Messrs. Hooker, manufacturers of screw twist drills.

He was an active member and deacon of the Good Will Congregational church, Syracuse, N. Y.

Copy of resolutions passed by Good Will S. S.:

"*To Dr. Wm. Manlius Smith and Family* :—

At the regular session of the Good Will Sunday School, Feb. 27, 1887, the following preamble and resolutions were adopted:

WHEREAS, Our Father having prepared a mansion and called to his heavenly home our brother, Dea. Azariah Smith, the members of Good Will Sunday School desire to make some expression of our love for him and our sorrow for all who held him dear; therefore, *Resolved*, that, although we know that our words are of no avail, we extend our sympathy to his family and pray that God may prove himself indeed a God of comfort and strength. *Resolved*, that while we realize our great loss as a Sunday school, we know that our brother has received infinite gain. He who lived among us such a beautiful life of prayer and trust is truly at home amid the glories of his Father's house, and there remains for us the memory and influence of his sweet example and the inspiration of the thought that his prayers and service are not interrupted but perfected. *Resolved*, That this testimonial be entered upon the school records and a copy sent to the family of our friend."

VI. Aulus Smith, son of Wm. Manlius, gr. son of Azariah, b. July 18, 1858, in Manlius, N. Y., graduated at the Union school in 1879, being chosen historian of his class. He became intensely interested in the art of printing, and soon after his graduation obtained a situation in the job office of the Syracuse

Daily Journal, and is now in the Eagle Printing House. He has studied phonography, and at one time purchased a type writer and did type-writing for the lawyers and business men of the city. He is passionately fond of music.

VII. Walter Storm Smith, son of Wm. Manlius, gr. son of Azariah, b. Feb. 7, 1860, in Manlius, N. Y., and d. Dec. 11, 1888. He was an expert chemist, pursued his studies under Prof. Goessman, at Amherst Agricultural College, Mass., in 1882 and '83, then returned to Syracuse and engaged in analytical chemical work in connection with Prof. F. E. Engelhardt till March, 1886, when Dr. E. became superintendent of salt works at Pifford, N. Y., and he carried on the work alone. About this time he was appointed Milk Inspector for the Health Board of the city of Syracuse, and continued in their employ till his death, after an illness of only a fortnight. He was unmarried and had always resided at home. He was an active member and supporter of the Good Will Congregational church of Syracuse, N. Y., and was librarian of the S. S. for years.

Copy of words of sympathy sent to Mr. and Mrs. Wm. M. Smith:

" Our Heavenly Father, in his wisdom and love, has called our brother, Walter S. Smith, home, as Jesus said, to be with Him where He is.

" We desire by this to express our sympathy with those who miss him from their household, and to tell of our love for him. He was among us full of love, cheerfulness and kindness, a follower of Jesus Christ. We remember him as ready for the Lord's work as it came before him and willing and earnest in doing it. He was one of those of whom we can say, ' He was faithful unto the end.' His work and influence shall remain with us and his memory is precious to us all.

THE GOOD WILL SUNDAY SCHOOL.

C. W. CABLE, Sec'y."

Copy of resolutions by the Y. P. S. C. E., to Dr. Wm. Manlius Smith and family:

" WHEREAS, It has pleased our Father in Heaven to call home our dear brother and friend, Walter S. Smith. *Resolved*, That it is but just to the memory of our departed friend to say that we shall miss him from our society because of his beautiful life and Christian example and faithful work. *Resolved*, That the Y. P. S. C. E. of Good Will church sincerely sympathize with the parents, brothers and sisters of the deceased in their afflictions.

JOHN K. DEAN,
President."

VIII. Newton Smith, son of Wm. Manlius, gr. son of Azariah, b. Aug. 21, 1862, in Manlius, N. Y., attended the Union school in Manlius, from which he graduated in 1879, and that fall entered the High school at Syracuse, N. Y., and in 1881 became a freshman at Syracuse University. In 1883 he left the university for the position of a bank clerk in Binghamton, N. Y., which position he held for over a year, when he left for a position in the office of Joseph P. Noyes & Co., Binghamton, N. Y., which position he still retains.

IX. Allen Macy Smith, son of Wm. Manlius, gr. son of Azariah, b. June 26, 1864, in Manlius, N. Y., graduated from Manlius Graded school, in June, 1880. In July, 1880, he took part in a competitive examination for scholarships to Cornell University, thaca, N. Y., and obtained a scholarship, but it was finally decided that he should not go to Cornell. He attended the High school in Syracuse for a year or two and the Syracuse University for about two years. In June, 1886, he graduated from Amherst College, Amherst, Mass., and from the Syracuse Medical College, at the head of his class, in June, 1889. He was recommended to Willard Asylum, Willard, N. Y., by Dr. Carson of the Syracuse Idiot Asylum and by Dr. Van Duyn of Syracuse, N.

Y., in whose office he spent considerable time during his course at the medical college. Soon after graduating from the medical college he went to Willard on a three months trial, passed a most excellent civil service medical examination, and at the end of three months was regularly appointed assistant physician there, where he is at present.

X. Clara Smith, dau. of Wm. Manlius, gr. dau. of Azariah, b. Feb. 5, 1866, in Manlius, N. Y., graduated from the Manlius Graded school of Manlius, N. Y., in June, 1881, and from the High school at Syracuse, N. Y., in January, 1884, and in June, 1887, from the Syracuse Medical College, at the head of her class. She went immediately to New York City, and for over a year had charge of the drug room at the dispensary of the " Woman's Infirmary for Women and Children," which work she did in a very satisfactory manner; while there saw considerable clinical practice. She returned to Syracuse in the summer of 1888, and for six months was in Dr. Didama's office. In April, 1889, she opened an office of her own in Syracuse, where she now is. She has been, so far, very successful and seems well fitted for the profession she has chosen.

XI. Louisa Smith, dau. of Wm. Manlius, gr. dau. of Azariah, b. July 18, 1868, in Manlius, N. Y., attended school in Manlius for some time, but did not remain and graduate, but entered the High school at Syracuse, N. Y., from which she graduated in January, 1885. She then took a course in the teachers' training class, and in June, 1886, began teaching. She taught her first year at East Syracuse, and at the close of that year was given a position in the Montgomery school in Syracuse, where she still is. She has always had charge of quite young children and seems peculiarly and especially adapted to that branch in the school, judging from the success which has attended her labors. She resides with her parents.

XII. Ludlow, son of Wm. Manlius, gr. son of Azariah, b. Aug. 7, 1870, in Manlius, N. Y., attended the schools in Manlius, and entered the High school in Syracuse and is a member of the graduating class this year, but on account of poor health has been obliged to leave school.

8. Zilpha Smith, dau. of Azariah, gr. dau. of Matthew 6th, b. April 1, 1825, in Manlius, N. Y., m. Mar. 5, 1845, Walter Storm, who was b. Sept. 3, 1820, in New Hamburgh, N. Y. At the age of eleven he went to New York City, where he was brought up a merchant. He was engaged there in the wholesale grocery business from 1842 to 1865, and in the tea trade after that until his death. After their marriage they resided a few years in New York, and then on Jersey City Heights until his death, which was Aug. 9, 1878, in Hinsdale, Mass. She received her education at Manlius Academy, and at Mrs. Willard's Seminary at Troy, N. Y. In 1890 she resided at Syracuse, N. Y.

CHILDREN:

I.—Azariah Smith, b. June 5, 1847.
II.—Clara Eleanor, b. Aug. 24, 1850.
III.—Daughter, b. Aug. 22, 1852, d. Aug. 24, 1852.
IV.—Son, b. July 17, 1854, d. July 28, 1854.
V.—Walter Lamont, b. April 10, 1856, d. Jan. 27, 1857.
VI.—James Bernard Bonnell, b. April 8, 1859, d. Jan. 16, 1863.
VII.—Bertrand, b. May 22, 1864.

Azariah Smith Storm, son of Zilpha, gr. son of Azariah, b. June 5, 1847, in Brooklyn, N. Y., m. Nov. 7, 1872, Emily Payne, who was b. Jan. 11, 1851, in Brighton, N. Y. He graduated at Williams College in 1870, and for several years was a tea merchant in New York City, and resided at Elizabeth, N. J., but now resides in Hinsdale, Mass., and is a commercial traveler.

CHILDREN:

I.—Mary Payne, b. June 17, 1873.
II.—Emily Zilpha, b. July 29, 1874.
III.—Katie Kittredge, b. Aug. 14, 1876.
IV.—Lyman Payne, b. Nov. 9, 1880, d. May 13, 1881.
V.—Mack Payne, b. May 23, 1888.

Clara Eleanor Storm, dau. of Zilpha, gr. dau. of Azariah, b. Aug. 24, 1850, in New York City, m. April 13 or 18, 1876, Charles S. Simpkins, who was b. May 22, 1847. He is a lawyer and they reside in Brooklyn, N. Y.

CHILDREN:

I.—Zilpha, b. Nov. 13, 1877, at Bergen, N. J.
II.—Annie A., b. Aug. 23, 1879, d. Nov. 22, 1886.
III.—Bessie, b. April 4, 1881, d. Aug. 5, 1881.
IV.—Charles Webster, b. Aug. 9, 1882.
V.—Bertrand D., b. July 13, 1884.
VI.—Edgar W., b. Feb. 26, 1886, d. July 18, 1886.
VII.—Frank McClellan, b. June 28, 1887.
VIII.—Leon T., b. April 1, 1889.

Bertrand Storm, son of Zilpha, gr. son of Azariah, b. May 22, 1864, at Bergen, N. J.; is now bookkeeper for a hardware firm in Syracuse, N. Y.

Descendants of Matthew Smith 7th.

V.

Matthew 7th, son of Matthew 6th, gr. son of Matthew 5th, b. Aug. 25, 1787, in Middlefield, Mass., m. Dec. 2, 1813, Betsey Ward, who was b. Jan. 25, 1794, in Chester, Mass., and d. Mar. 21, 1867, at the home of her oldest daughter, in Watervliet, Michigan. He d. Mar. 20, 1855, in Middlefield, Mass. He was a prosperous farmer, and for many years justice of the peace and selectman in Middlefield, and his sound judgment and sterling worth commanded universal confidence and respect.

CHILDREN:

I.—Matthew, b. Sept. 13, 1814.
II.—John. b. Mar. 18, 1816.
III.—Eliza, b. April 29, 1818.
IV.—Asenath, b. Sept. 9, 1820.
V.—Azariah, b. Dec. 2, 1822, d. Oct. 12, 1827.
VI.—Benjamin Franklin, b. June 17, 1825, d. April 18, 1826.
VII.—Mary Ann, b. April 9, 1828, d. Nov. 1, 1831.
VIII.—Sally, b. April 19, 1830.
IX.—Mary Ann 2d, b. Aug. 13, 1832.
X.—Elmira Ward, b. Dec. 28, 1834, and d. Sept. 7, 1850.

1. Matthew 8th, son of Matthew 7th, gr. son of Matthew 6th, b. Sept. 13, 1814, in Middlefield, Mass., m. Mar. 15, 1840, Maria Delight Root, who was b. December 31, 1817, in Middlefield, Mass. She was second child of Capt. Solomon Root and Laura (Mack) Root. She d. Feb. 14, 1883, at the house of her daughter in Huntington, Mass. Matthew spent his boyhood days on the farm, was engaged in teaching many years, was

one of the board of selectmen and in 1878 represented his district in the Legislature. He is a man of public spirit, was chiefly instrumental in the formation of the Highland Agricultural Society, and donated the land which is used as their fair ground. He has been a merchant and a farmer. About 1885 he gave up his home in Middlefield, and since then has resided with his oldest daughter in Cheyenne, Wyoming.

CHILDREN: (all born in Middlefield, Mass.)

I.—Infant son, b. June 15, 1841, d. June 18, 1841.
II.—Infant son, b. Sept. 22, 1842, d. Sept. 26, 1842.
III.—Helen Maria, b. Dec. 9, 1843.
IV.—Eliza Ann, b. May 20, 1846.
V.—Matthew, b. Sept. 15, 1848.
VI.—Emma, b. April 17, 1851, d. Dec. 27, 1856.
VII.—Charles Sumner, b. May 27, 1856.

Four of the children lived to mature years, but Matthew, who was Matthew 9th in *direct descent*, d. Jan. 1, 1871, and was unmarried.

Helen Maria Smith, dau. of Matthew 8th, gr. dau. of Matthew 7th, b. Dec. 9, 1843, in Middlefield, Mass., m. Jan. 26, 1871, Francis Emroy Warren, who was b. June 20, 1844, in Hinsdale, Mass., and resided there and in adjoining towns until 1868. His younger days were spent on a farm and in the school room until the outbreak of the civil war, when he enlisted in Company C, Forty-ninth Regiment Mass. Volunteers. The self-possession, culture and bravery which have since characterized his success in business life secured his promotion to the position of captain in the Massachusetts militia, to which he was appointed by Gov. John A. Andrew. When but twenty-three years of age he went to Des Moines, Iowa, and in June, 1868, to Cheyenne, Wyoming. He took a position as clerk in the business of which he has since acquired the ownership. In public life he has held many prominent offices in the territory, and has had the best of opportunities of familiarizing himself with the territory's affairs and needs. He has been territorial treasurer, presiding officer of the higher branch of the Legislature and twice a member and chairman of the Republican central committee. He has been a member of the city council and was mayor of Cheyenne, when, on Feb. 25, 1885, President Arthur appointed him governor, which position he occupied twenty-one months. His record in the executive's chair is one to which any man might point with pride. His opposition to the Sparks land policy, which has since been execrated by every intelligent man of both parties, resulted in his removal. His prompt action in suppressing the Chinese riots in the Rock Springs coal mines stamped him as a man of courage and executive ability. March 26, 1889, President Harrison reappointed him governor, and there was great rejoicing in the territory, not confined to any political party. He is the most popular man in Wyoming, among Democrats and Republicans alike. To-day he owns cattle and sheep ranches, the gas works and electric light works and several business blocks. He is president of the Cheyenne board of trade and of the F. E. Warren Mercantile Co. Since Wyoming became a State he has been re-elected governor and on Nov. 18, 1890, was elected U. S. senator.

CHILDREN:

I.—Helen Frances, b. Aug. 16, 1880, in Cheyenne, Wyoming.
II.—Frederick Emroy, b. Jan. 20, 1884, " "

Eliza Ann Smith, dau. of Matthew 8th, gr. dau. of Matthew 7th, b. May 20, 1846, in Middlefield, Mass., m. Nov. 21, 1871, Henry Ellsworth Stanton, who was b. Jan. 23, 1846, in Huntington, Mass. He was a volunteer in the late war, and after his return worked at his trade, which was that of carriage maker, one year, then engaged in the grain and lumber business, and at present is carrying on the latter at Huntington, Mass. He has been unfortunate, as the dams built were not enduring enough to resist the mighty torrent which the Westfield river becomes during the oft-recurring freshets which occur during the rainy seasons and when the ice breaks up in the spring and goes out with irresistible force, but in 1875 he built a dam that has withstood the pressure. Not only does he saw rough lumber, but almost to an extreme the waste slabs are utilized, making lath, bed slats, whip butts, frost blocks, shingles, cattle stanchions, etc. He has all the latest improvements in machinery, and is carrying on a large business.

CHILDREN:

I.—Emroy Ellsworth, b. June 30, 1873, in Huntington, Mass.
II.—Robert Henry, b. May 7, 1875, in Middlefield, Mass., and d. Sept. 27, 1877, in Huntington, Mass.
III.—Luke Winchell, b. April 22, 1879, in Huntington, Mass.

Charles Sumner Smith (afterwards changed to Charles Matthew Smith), son of Matthew 8th, gr. son of Matthew 7th, b. May 27, 1856, in Middlefield, Mass., m. Mar. 20, 1883, Laura Parks, who was b. June 5, 1860, and d. June 2, 1890. He attended schools in Middlefield and Worcester, Mass., was a clerk at Gill's art and book store, Springfield, Mass.; also engaged in the grain business, carrying on a gristmill at Huntington, Mass. About 1880 he went to Cheyenne, Wyoming, and is now a member of the firm, "The Warren Mercantile Co." They have no children except an adopted son, Parks, a nephew of Mrs. Smith.

In the Cheyenne Daily Leader of June 3d is the following: "The people of Cheyenne were startled yesterday by the report of the death of Mrs. Chas. M. Smith. Comparatively few people were aware of her illness and none appreciated its dangerous character. During their residence in this city Mrs. Smith had made for herself a host of friends. Charming in manner and person, well read and sprightly in disposition, a superb hostess and entertainer, she won her way into the affections of all her acquaintances. Her disposition was at all times affable and unaffected. There was a charm in her manner and a warmth in her greeting which gave outward evidence of her kindly disposition and personification to the poet's lines:

> 'None knew her but to love her,
> None named her but to praise.'

"A fitting tribute was paid to her by the literary circle of which she was the respected president.

"At a called meeting of the Beta Social Literary circle of this city the following resolutions were adopted:

"WHEREAS, It has pleased our all-wise and loving Father to remove Mrs. Laura P. Smith, beloved president of the Beta Social Literary circle, to the circle of the redeemed and crowned in heaven,

"*Resolved*, That we express our heartfelt sympathy to the bereaved husband and relatives in this unexpected and deep affliction, and testify to the virtues, graces and accomplishments of our president. Words are weak to convey our sense of personal loss. Mrs. Smith was, by her simple, charming and affable manners, one of the most lovable of persons, unaffected and sincere in her friendship.

"*Resolved*, That these resolutions be transmitted to the husband of the deceased as a token of our love for her, and that the newspapers of the city be each supplied with a copy.

"The funeral was held at the Baptist church on her 30th birthday. The immediate cause of her death was probably peritonitis. Although she had not been in robust health for several years she was not an invalid by any means, and her death was as peaceful as the sinking of a tired child to rest."

2. John, son of Matthew 7th, gr. son of Matthew 6th, b. Mar. 18, 1816, in Middlefield, Mass., m. May 19, 1841, Elvira Root, who was b. Sept. 24, 1819, in Richmond, Mass. She was third child of Capt Solomon Root and Laura (Mack) Root. In 1890 she resided with her daughter in Hartford, Conn. John

spent his early life on the farm. He taught school in Middlefield and Chester, Mass., and Huntington, Long Island. In Middlefield, Mass., he was town clerk, justice of the peace and member of the school committee. When in Becket, Mass., in the lumber business, he was justice of the peace and two years was a member of the Legislature. In Boston, Mass., he was salesman in the clothing store of L. D. Boise. In Fair Haven, Vermont, he resided fifteen years, for ten years being agent for the Scotch Hill Slate Co., manufacturers of roofing slate. In 1881 he removed to Middlefield, Mass. "He was a faithful, earnest Christian and for many years an active member of the Baptist church. As a wise counsellor and faithful friend he was one who commanded respect from all who knew him." He d. Sept. 3, 1885, in Northampton, Mass.

CHILDREN: (all born in Middlefield, Mass.)

I.—John Henry, b. July 12, 1842.
II.—Sophia, b. April 21, 1847.
III.—Mary Ann, b. Oct. 20, 1851, and d. Oct. 20, 1851.

John Henry Smith, son of John, gr. son of Matthew 7th, b. July 12, 1842, in Middlefield, Mass., m. April 8, 1873, Mrs. Sarah Eveline Parks (*née* Aborn), who was b. Oct. 14, 1840, in Lincoln, Vermont. He served in the civil war in the 47th Mass. Reg. Volunteers, and was clerk in grocery stores in Middlefield and Newton, Mass., and Fair Haven, Vt., and there went into the business on his own account, and has since continued in it, moving in 1881 to his present home in Dalton, Mass., where he has been chairman of the selectmen, one of the assessors and a member of the board of health.

CHILDREN:

I.—Sophia Elvira, b. Jan. 28, 1875, in Fair Haven, Vermont.

Sophia Smith, dau. of John, gr. dau. of Matthew 7th, b. April 21, 1847, in Middlefield, Mass., m. Nov. 1, 1887, Thomas Martin (son of Anna (Smith) Martin, gr. son of Matthew Smith 6th), who was b. Aug. 29, 1818, in Washington, Mass., and now (1890) resides in Hartford, Conn. (For account of his life see previous account in " Descendants of Anna Smith.")

She received her education in the Chapman Grammar school, and Girls' High and Normal school in Boston, Mass., and in 1866, began teaching in the public schools of Fair Haven, Vermont, teaching nearly nine years, then was bookkeeper for the F. H. Marble and Marbleized Slate Co. nearly two years. Spent one year (1878) in Middlefield, Mass., and prepared the " Mack Genealogy," which was published in 1879, in Vermont. With her parents (being needed at home) she removed in 1881 to Middlefield, Mass., and in November, 1886, with her mother to Huntington, Mass., where she resided (one year) until her marriage, when the home was sold and her mother went to Hartford, Conn., to live with her. She commenced the " Smith Genealogy " in 1878, and sincerely hopes it will be prized by future generations if not by the present.

Her address is 792 Main street, Hartford, Conn., and she would be pleased at *any time* to hear of any changes in any family, or anything about *any person* mentioned in this book.

No children.

3. Eliza, dau. of Matthew 7th, gr. dau. of Matthew 6th, b. April 29, 1818, in Middlefield, Mass., m. Sept. 3, 1839, Elias Thompson Spencer, who was b. Aug. 11, 1815, in Middlefield, Mass. He is a farmer and resides in Watervliet, Mich.

CHILDREN:

I.—Eliza Ann, b. Sept. 8, 1841.
II.—Lucy F., b. Oct. 9, 1843.
III.—Julia H., b. Aug. 25, 1852.
IV.—Elmira Asenath, b. Aug. 14, 1860.

Eliza Ann Spencer, dau. of Eliza, gr. dau. of Matthew 7th, b. Sept. 8, 1841, in Farmington, Ohio, m. 1st, June 29, 1861, James M. Burke, who was b. Mar. 7, 1832, in North Adams, Mass., and d. July 17, 1875. She m. 2d, Aug. 31, 1879, Daniel Coleman Johnson, who was b. April 6, 1835. They reside in Watervliet, Michigan.

CHILDREN : (by 1st marriage.)

I.—Myrtie M., b. May 13, 1862.
II.—Jessie G., b. Jan. 4, 1864.
III.—Mervin H., b. April 25, 1869; is an assistant book-keeper and corresponding clerk in a wholesale agricultural house in Burlington, Iowa.
IV.—Arvin S., b. Jan. 2, 1875, d. May 17, 1877.

(by 2d marriage.)

V.—Irene, b. Oct. 24, 1881.
VI.—Loraine, b. Feb. 27, 1883.

Myrtie M. Burke, dau. of Eliza Ann, gr. dau. of Eliza, b. May 13, 1862, m. 1st, Mar. 10, 1883, Charles M. Dobson, who was b. Sept. 13, 1861, and d. Feb. 20, 1887. She m. 2d, Oct. 1, 1889, Truman H. Wadhams, who was b. Jan. 23, 1855. They reside at Mount Pleasant, Michigan.

CHILDREN : (by 1st marriage.)

I.—George Burke, b. Nov. 25, 1883.

Jessie G. Burke, dau. of Eliza Ann, gr. dau. of Eliza, b. Jan. 4, 1864, m. Mar. 31, 1886, Abel M. Burns, who was b. Dec. 29, 1863.

CHILDREN:

I.—Orpha Viola, b. Feb. 3, 1887.
II.—Harrison Arvin, b. Oct. 22, 1888.

Lucy F. Spencer, dau. of Eliza, gr. dau. of Matthew 7th, b. Oct. 9, 1843, in Atwater, Ohio, m. Nov. 10, 1861, Nelson R. Bonfoey, who was b. Feb. 17, 1827, in Richfield, N. Y. They reside in Watervliet, Michigan.

CHILDREN:

I.—Lizzie A., b. Feb. 28, 1867.
II.—Nora H., b. July 22, 1874, d. June 26, 1877.
III.—Freeman, b. Sept. 21, 1881.

Lizzie A. Bonfoey, dau. of Lucy, gr. dau. of Eliza, b. Feb. 28, 1867, m. May 5, 1886, Worden G. Barnaby, who was b. Oct. 10, 1858, in Ulysses, Pa. He resides in Hudsonville, Michigan, where he has exclusive charge of the R. R. station.

CHILDREN:

I.—Olive Lucy, b. Sept. 16, 1887.

Julia H. Spencer, dau. of Eliza, gr. dau. of Matthew 7th, b. Aug. 25, 1852, in Cleveland, Ohio, m. May 7, 1874, Wm. W. Knapp, who was b. May 14, 1853, in Hartford, Michigan. They reside in Watervliet, Michigan.
No children.

Elmira Asenath Spencer, dau. of Eliza, gr. dau. of Matthew 7th, b. Aug. 14, 1860, in Watervliet, Michigan, m. Oct. 18, 1882, Charles C. Knapp (brother of Wm. W. Knapp), who was

b. July 6, 1860, in Watervliet, Michigan. She d. Dec. 4, 1889. They resided in Winterville, Missouri. Two weeks previous to her death she, with her husband and child, had come to Watervliet, Mich., to visit relatives and friends. She was away visiting for the day when stricken with paralysis, and died after a sickness of only two hours.

CHILDREN:

I.—Frankie Myra, b. Nov. 5, 1883, d. Aug. 25, 1885.
II.—Lucia Eva, b. April 26, 1885, in Browning, Mo.
III.—Mabel, b. Nov. 27, 1887, in Winterville, Mo., and d. there, Jan. 8, 1888.

4. Asenath Smith, dau. of Matthew 7th, gr. dau. of Matthew 6th, b. Sept. 9, 1820, in Middlefield, Mass., m. Oct. 30, 1844, Elisha Strong (of Northampton, Mass.), who was b. Oct. 26, 1820, and d. May 17, 1890. She d. May 5, 1855.

CHILDREN:

I.—Ellen Ward, b. April 5, 1846.
II.—Infant daughter, b. Feb. 28, 1849, d. Mar. 4, 1849.
III.—Elisha, b. Dec. 20, 1853, d. Aug. 22, 1854.
IV.—Elisha, b. April 19, 1855, d. Feb. 13, 1861.

Ellen Ward Strong, dau. of Asenath, gr. dau. of Matthew 7th, b. April 5, 1846, m. Jan. 12, 1869, Luther A. Clark, who was b. Nov. 2, 1838. They have always lived in Northampton, Mass.

CHILDREN:

I.—Elisha Luther, b. April 9, 1870, in Northampton, Mass., and d. July 13, 1887, in Chelsea, Mass. He was a member of the High School, an unusually fine scholar, a most excellent penman, and had for the first time been away alone from his parents, spending his vacation. He was suddenly stricken down with diphtheria, having been gone from home but a week.

8. Sally, dau. of Matthew 7th, gr. dau. of Matthew 6th, b. April 19, 1830, in Middlefield, Mass., m. Nov. 9, 1854, Charles Wright, who was b. Dec. 8, 1830, and d. Sept. 20, 1889. He was a farmer and had always lived in Middlefield, Mass., where he had served his day and generation in various ways, as church clerk for thirty years, S. S. superintendent, school committee and selectman.

CHILDREN:

I.—Elsie Adelaide, b. Aug. 19, 1855.
II.—Wm. Smith, b. June 13, 1859, in Middlefield, Mass., but since 1881 has resided in Dalton, Mass., where he first engaged as clerk, but is now one of the firm of Smith & Wright.
III.—Helen Maria, b. Feb. 9, 1873, in Middlefield, Mass., where she still resides with her mother, being a successful teacher.

Elsie Adelaide Wright, dau. of Sally, gr. dau. of Matthew 7th, b. Aug. 19, 1855, in Middlefield, Mass., m. May 8, 1879, George W. Cottrell, who was b. Mar. 15, 1856, in Hinsdale, Mass. He is a farmer, resides in Middlefield, Mass., and is credited with making the purest and best maple sugar in that vicinity.

CHILDREN:

I.—Mary Adelaide, b. Feb. 14, 1881.
II.—Frank Arthur, b. Aug. 8, 1882.
III.—Sarah Elsie, b. Mar. 7, 1884.
IV.—John, b. Nov. 20, 1888.

9. Mary Ann, dau. of Matthew 7th, gr. dau. of Matthew 6th, gt. gr. dau. of Matthew 5th, b. Aug. 13, 1832, in Middlefield, Mass., m. April 7, 1857, Albert Smith (son of Ebenezer, gr. son of Calvin, gt. gr. son of Matthew 5th), who was b. Sept. 30, 1832, in Middlefield, Mass. He is a farmer (though now out of health), and resides in Elgin, Illinois.

CHILDREN:

I.—Ella Florence, b. Mar. 20, 1859, d. Jan. 19, 1886, of consumption. She had been sick about three years, and her many good qualities had endeared her to a large circle of friends.

II.—Albert Matthew, b. April 4, 1863, m. Sept. 30, 1884, Clara Stringer, who was b. June 17, 1861. He is a farmer in Elgin, Illinois.

CHILDREN:

1. Edwin Harold, b. Mar. 31, 1887, d. April 22, 1889.
2. Albert Leo, b. August 3, 1890.

III.—Carrie Birdie, dau. of Albert and Mary Ann Smith, b. Mar. 29, 1873, d. June 26, 1873.

Descendants of Joseph Smith.

VI.

Joseph Smith, son of Matthew 6th, gr. son of Matthew 5th, b. Sept. 28, 1789, in Middlefield, Mass., m. Dec. 13, 1815, Sophia Wattles, who was b. March 1, 1798, in Lebanon, Conn., and d. May 1, 1839, in Manlius, N. Y. He d. Jan. 22, 1849, in Manlius, N. Y.

CHILDREN:

I.—Joseph, b. Sept. 19, 1816, d. Jan. 6, 1841.

II.—Daniel Wattles, b. Dec. 29, 1819, m. July 25, 1844, Mrs. Mary S. Root, (*née* Smith), who was b. in 1820, and d. Jan. 10, 1874, at Glen Cove, N. Y. He d. at Manlius, N. Y., Dec. 19, 1852. No children.

III.—Sophia, b. Jan. 13, 1822, at Manlius, N. Y., m. May 12, 1842, Hiram Remington, who was b. Mar. 2, 1816, and is still living. She d. July 29, 1844, in Manlius, N. Y. No children.

IV.—James Otis, b. July 23, 1826, at Manlius, N. Y., and d. at same place, Mar. 20, 1829.

V.—Ann Augusta, b. Mar. 7, 1831, m. Jan. 30, 1866, John Henry Rowling, who was b. Jan. 3, 1831, and d. Mar. 10, 1873, at Cool Well, Va. After his death she conducted kindergarten schools and is now in New York. No children.

Descendants of Samuel Smith.

—:o:—

IX.

Samuel Smith, son of Matthew 6th, grandson of Matthew 5th, b. Aug. 28, 1797, in Middlefield, Mass., m. July 10, 1822, Lucina Metcalf (dau. of John Metcalf), who was b. Aug. 9, 1799, in Middlefield, Mass., and d. May 5, 1859.

He was for many years one of the Board of Selectmen and Assessors of Middlefield; also a leading member of the School Committee. He represented his town in the Legislature of Massachusetts for the year 1839.

Before his marriage, and for some years after, he was a teacher of marked success and renown in his own and in the neighboring towns. He was naturally a most assiduous reader and a most enthusiastic student, and maintained these characteristics through all his life.

He connected himself with the Baptist church in 1832, and was always a liberal supporter of the pecuniary burdens of the church and an habitual attendant upon its public worship.

All the children and grandchildren gathered at the old home on his completing his eightieth year, and spent a delightful season in reminiscences and mutual intercourse.

One short month later the summons came and found him ready; and he came to his "grave in a full age, like as a shock of corn cometh in in his season." He d. Sept. 27, 1877.

CHILDREN: (all born in Middlefield, Mass.)

I.—Lucy, b. July 9, 1823.
II.—Sarah, b. Oct. 1, 1824.
III.—Samuel, b. Aug. 5, 1826.
IV.—Anna, b. July 24, 1828.
V.—John Metcalf, b. Sept. 7, 1830.

VI.—Azariah, b. Jan'y 12, 1833.
VII.—Joseph, ⎞ b. Mar. 25, 1835.
VIII.—James, ⎠ b. Mar. 25, 1835, d. Aug. 1, 1838.
IX.—Judson, b. June 28, 1837.
X.—Edward Payson, b. Jan'y 20, 1840.

1. Lucy Smith, dau. of Samuel, granddau. of Matthew 6th, b. July 9, 1823, in Middlefield, Mass., m. Nov. 28, 1867, Ambrose Newton, who was b. June 11, 1800, and d. Feb'y 28, 1878. He was a farmer. She was a graduate of Mount Holyoke Seminary, and for many years was a teacher, teaching in Middlefield and Pittsfield, Mass., Honesdale, Pa., and Brandon, Vermont. When her mother's health failed she assumed the care of the home, looked after her brothers in their courses of study, and performed for them all a measureless labor of love. She lives in Middlefield.

No children.

2. Sarah Smith, dau. of Samuel, granddau. of Matthew 6th, b. Oct. 1, 1824, in Middlefield, Mass., m. June 18, 1856, DeWitt Gardner, who was b. Mar. 28, 1819, in Cazenovia, N. Y.

She graduated at Mount Holyoke Seminary in 1843, and was for a dozen years a teacher in private schools in Norwich, Conn., and Walthourville, Ga., and as preceptress in Onondaga Academy, N. Y.

Mr. Gardner has resided in Fulton, N. Y., since he was seventeen years of age, commencing business life as a clerk, then becoming a successful merchant, and in 1855 was made cashier of the Oswego River, now First National Bank, which position he still retains. He has also built up a flourishing milling business and is head partner in the firm, Gardner & Seymour, St. Louis Mills.

He is highly esteemed for his unswerving integrity, honesty and conscientious devotion to duty, and has been for fifty years a consistent member of the Presbyterian Church.

CHILDREN:

Alice May, b. Dec. 12, 1861,
A graduate of Oberlin College and an artist.

3. Samuel Smith, son of Samuel, grandson of Matthew 6th, b. Aug. 5, 1826, in Middlefield, Mass., m. Sept. 25, 1851, Mary Maria Bliss, who was b. Jan'y 17, 1827.

He pursued his higher studies in Williston Seminary, graduating in the scientific course in 1846. He taught in public schools a few terms, and then purchased a farm in Middlefield. In 1867 he removed to Amherst, Mass., where he resided in 1890.

CHILDREN: (all born in Middlefield, Mass.)

I.—Grace Tallulah, b. Sept. 17, 1852, d. Feb'y 2, 1855, in Middlefield, Mass.
II.—Hosea Bliss, b. Feb'y 4, 1856.
III.—Percy Lee, b. Sept. 24, 1861.
IV.—Ernest Bliss, b. Dec. 8, 1863.

Hosea B. Smith, son of Samuel, grandson of Samuel, b. Feb'y 4, 1856, in Middlefield, Mass., m. Feb'y 4, 1879, Una Josephine Carr, who was b. Dec. 4, 1859, in Lyndon, Vermont.

He is a farmer in Amherst, Mass.

CHILDREN : (all born in Amherst, Mass.)

I.—Edwin Ray, b. Mar. 20, 1880.
II.—Percy Clayton, b. Feb. 7, 1885.

Percy Lee Smith, son of Samuel, gr. son of Samuel, b. Sept. 24, 1861, in Middlefield, Mass., and is in business at Cheyenne, Wyoming.

4. Anna Smith, dau. of Samuel, granddau. of Matthew 6th, b. July 24, 1828, in Middlefield, Mass., m. Jan'y 1, 1850, Solomon Francis Root, who was b. Aug. 31, 1826, in Middlefield, Mass.

She pursued her higher studies at Mount Holyoke Female Seminary, not, however, completing the course. She was an acceptable teacher in the public schools for several terms. She died Mar. 24, 1874, in Boston, at the home of her brother, whither she had gone for medical relief. Mr. Root, while in Middlefield, held the office of Town Treasurer and Justice of the Peace, and in Russell, Mass., was Town Clerk and a member of the School Committee. He is a merchant, and in 1878 (having again married in 1876), resided in Dalton, Mass., having a store there, also one in Hinsdale, Mass. In 1881 he removed to E. Douglas, Mass., where he at present is a merchant.

CHILDREN: (all born in Middlefield, Mass.)

I.—James Francis, b. Sept. 24, 1850, d. May 23, 1866, in Middlefield.
II.—Azariah Smith, b. Feb. 3, 1862.

Azariah Smith Root, son of Anna, grandson of Samuel, b. Feb. 3, 1862, in Middlefield, Mass., m. April 30, 1887, Anna Mayo Metcalf of Elyria, Ohio, who was b. July 26, 1862, in Elyria. He prepared for college at Middlefield Select School, High Schools of Hinsdale and Pittsfield, Mass., and the preparatory department of Oberlin College, where he graduated in the classical course, June, 1884, and received the degree of A. M. in June, 1887. Studied law at the Boston University Law School and Harvard Law School. He was invited to catalogue the library of Oberlin College, Ohio, and had been employed sixteen months in that work when he was appointed Librarian, Feb. 3, 1887. He is editor of the Triennial Catalogue of Alumni, Secretary of the Society of Alumni of Oberlin College, a member and Librarian of the Ohio Church History Society, and a member of the American Library Association.

CHILDREN:

I.—Francis Metcalf, b. Sept. 24, 1889.

5. John Metcalf Smith, son of Samuel, grandson of Matthew 6th, b. Sept. 7, 1830, in Middlefield, Mass., m. Dec. 30, 1857, Harriet Louise Eldredge (dau. of Lyman Eldredge, M. D., of Cincinnatus, N. Y.), who was b. May 31, 1835.

He pursued his preparatory studies in Springfield and Easthampton, Mass., and his collegiate studies in New York Central College, where he graduated in 1855. He was immediately appointed to the Professorship of Mixed Mathematics and Natural Sciences in Central College, where he remained till November, 1857. He then accepted the same chair in Eleutherian College, Indiana, and taught there two years; was then principal of Lewistown Academy, Mifflin county, Pa., for three years, and principal of the High School in Collinsville, Conn., for two years. In 1864 he came back with his family to the old home in Middlefield, to relieve his father of care, and in 1890 resided there, having had countless public duties and services in teaching and in town affairs.

CHILDREN:

I.—Sophie Adelphia, b. Jan. 20, 1861.
II.—Theodore Winthrop, b. Nov. 9, 1862, d. Oct 24, 1865, in Middlefield.
III.—Infant daughter, b. Jan. 21, 1867, d. Jan. 21, 1867, in Middlefield.
IV.—Gerald Birney, b. May 3, 1868. In 1890 at Brown University.
V.—Louis Carter, b. Mar. 3, 1870. In 1890 at Worcester Technical Institute.
VI.—Kate Winifred, b. Sept. 25, 1871. In 1890 at Mount Holyoke Seminary.
VII.—Edward Cecil, b. Dec. 15, 1873, d. April 2, 1889, at Middlefield. He was an exceptionally promising youth.
VIII.—Samuel Eldredge, b. Oct. 25, 1877.

Sophie Adelphia Smith, dau. of John M., granddau. of Samuel, b. Jan. 20, 1861, in Lewistown, Pa., m. Jan. 30, 1887 (in San Francisco, Cal.), Rev. Arthur William Burt (a graduate of Oberlin), who was b. April 3, 1855, in Kent, Ohio.

As soon as married they started on the Selina, with six other passengers, for Hilo, Hawaiian Islands, and in the Hawaiian Gazette, Feb. 22, 1887, was found the following:

"WRECK OF THE SELINA."

"Friday, Feb. 11, twelve days from San Francisco, with a full cargo of merchandise, cows, mules, hogs and six passengers. On coming into the harbor, just at dark, she was cast upon the rocks, under the high bluff, one-half mile from Waimaker Sugar Mill, and became a total wreck. By a miracle, almost, the passengers and all on board were saved, but they had to be drawn through the surf and helped up the almost perpendicular bluff, over 100 ft. high, to *terra firma*, and thence conveyed by foot men and on horseback over the worst possible of roads, mud almost waist deep, for at least half a mile, to a place where carriages could be taken.

"The anchors were both cast out when it was found the Selina was drifting, but both chains parted and a sudden squall threw the brig upon the rocks a ship's length from the strand, with the breakers dashing furiously over the ship at dark, 6:30 P. M. The first idea of accident to the Selina that any one at Hilo had was when the whistle blew at Waimaker's, but it was so dark that nothing could be seen, save the running to and fro of lights on the shore. Soon after a gun was fired as a signal of distress, followed by a second, which told the Hiloites that there certainly was trouble and help was needed. For some days the surf had been very high, and as the Selina came along it was found that her passengers could not land at the wharf. The club boat went off to the Selina and Mr. Awai, the custom house officer, took passage in it. After the Selina anchored (it being about dark), the club boat left and pulled for the shore, which was reached (with the boat full of water) about 7 o'clock. The Hiloites had sent for boats to Warkea, and issued an order to Judge Lyman to call on all the vessels in the harbor for help. An attempt was also made to get the little steamer, Ivy Holmes, but she was out of repair. All Hilo was astir. Soon word arrived that Awai had jumped overboard and swam for the shore, but the task was more than he supposed, and after being beaten about by the waves, he was dragged ashore more dead than alive, and was brought into Hilo, to his home. For two hours all on board were being wet and thrown down by the waves that constantly dashed in fury over the vessel, throwing down all who attempted to stand. In time ropes were rigged from the shore to the ship, and the passengers and crew, one by one, were drawn through the breakers to the shore, where they were cared for by willing hands. By ten o'clock the ship was entirely deserted. During the night the sea went down considerably and an attempt was made on Saturday to save the freight on board. The passengers' baggage was all recovered, but in a wretched condition, everything being soaked with water, and a great portion ruined. The live stock, such as had not been killed by falling masts, were taken through the breakers to boats lying some distance off (no boats dared come near the wreck), and thus conveyed to Hilo. Before all were off, the ship was found to be on fire, the slaking lime having caught the kerosene in the hold. The hatches were taken off and the flames burst forth with fury. The hatches were replaced to smother the fire, and the hogs were thrown overboard to make their own way through the breakers. By Sunday morning a hose pipe had been found and a flume built to the edge of the bluff, and water poured into the ship and the fire subdued. Monday morning the brig was sold at auction for $110.00. Tuesday the Selina was again found to be on fire, but little could be saved from the wreck except in a very damaged condition.

"Monday, Awai, the C. H. officer, was around, hunting up the shipwrecked passengers and demanding from each the $2.00 hospital tax, the fee required to enter the kingdom.

"What are the Hilo police good for? They were stationed, Friday night, to watch the wreck and to prevent all stealing, but instead of doing their duty, they at least seemed to connive at the thieving. Portuguese and natives vied with each other as to who would steal the most. Passengers' baggage was taken as well as other things; cases of goods were opened and taken away; natives were found wearing the apparel of the passengers; hundreds of dollars worth of property was taken, and yet not an arrest."

LIST OF PASSENGERS.

Rev. and Mrs. A. W. Burt, Hilo, Boarding School.
Mrs. George Paty and child, Hilo.
Mrs. Harris, Mrs. Gillen, Miss Low, San Francisco.
Mr. McChesney, Honolulu.

Mrs. Burt, in writing to her friends, spoke of their trying to get ashore in boats, and then spoke of the rope fastened to the ship and a huge rock on the shore, and the passengers would take hold of this rope and slide their hands along while they were pulled along by a smaller rope around their bodies, drawn by those on shore. The sea being rough, the ship would sway, making some of the time the rope slack, so they were a part of the time in the water and part of the time out. As they were landed under a precipice 150 feet high, they had to be drawn up by ropes around their waists, some of the distance perpendicular, and a part of the way they could help themselves a little, but were terribly bruised and scratched on the rocks. Mrs. Burt lost one barrel (that was burned) of books and bedding, and what was saved, was in a damaged condition, many of her valuables being so badly water-soaked as to be entirely worthless.

Mr. Burt's father being killed in a battle in the War of the Rebellion, he was obliged, when quite young, to take care of himself, working on farms for a time, then learned the carpenter's trade. At the age of twenty-three began a course of study at Oberlin, and graduated in 1882, and then took a theological course and graduated in 1885, then was pastor at Riverside (a suburb of Cincinnati), Ohio, one year. His health failing he resigned and decided to try the climate of the Sandwich Islands, where he went in May, 1886, and the following September began as principal of the Hilo boarding school. Since he has been there he has added an industrial school, built a large shop, with water power, and placed in it considerable machinery, so that the boys are learning considerable in the mechanic arts.

CHILDREN:

I.—Arthur Winthrop, b. June 11, 1888, in Hilo.

6. Azariah Smith, son of Samuel, gr. son of Matthew 6th, b. Jan. 12, 1833, in Middlefield, Mass., m. Sept. 25, 1861, Sophia Elizabeth Van Duzer of Silver Creek, N. Y., who was b. Feb. 19, 1839.

For thirteen years he spent the summers on the farm (early learning that even small hands could find something to do), and the winters in the little school house near his home. Thanks to good teachers and the helpful encouragement of his parents, he gained so fair a mastery of the branches taught in common schools that a few months in the Academy at Manlius, N. Y., and two terms at Williston Seminary, Easthampton, Mass., supplemented by a term under the tuition of his brother Metcalf, enabled him to enter New York Central College, McGrawville, N. Y., with his brother Metcalf, in the autumn of 1851. His father chose that college because of its liberal character, which made no discrimination against sex or color. Immediately on graduating, in 1855, he was elected Professor of Greek and librarian in the college, and continued there until November, 1857. Then he taught a year in Kishacoquillas Seminary, in Mifflin Co., Pennsylvania, and from 1859 to 1863 was superintendent of schools for that county. From June, 1863, to June, 1865, he was cashier in the United States military telegraph service at Nashville, Tenn. In September, 1865, he became connected with the book-publishing house of Ticknor & Fields, Boston, Mass., and has continued with their successors, Fields, Osgood & Co., James R. Osgood & Co., Houghton, Osgood & Co., and Houghton, Mifflin & Co., having charge of the publishing department.

CHILDREN:

I.—Rupert Van Duzer, b. Feb. 10, 1868, d. May 31, 1869.
II.—Theodore Clarke, b. May 18, 1870. (In 1890 in Harvard College.)
III.—Florence Elizabeth, b. June 6, 1873. (In 1890 in Smith College.)

7. Joseph Smith, son of Samuel, gr. son of Matthew 6th, b. Mar. 25, 1835 (a twin), in Middlefield, Mass., m. Dec. 13, 1876, Annie M. French (daughter of Capt. H. W. French of Hyde Park, Mass.), who was b. Oct. 20, 1848, in Stockton, Maine.

He d. in Boston, Mass., Feb. 20, 1879. He pursued his higher studies at New York Central College, and was an acceptable teacher in public schools for several terms. He early chose the mercantile profession and entered upon his career in Boston, with the firm of Bemis, Boise & Co., wholesale clothiers. He continued in this business, being a partner in the firm of Knowles, Leland & Co., until 1879, when he engaged in the manufacture of gold rings, being a member of the firm of Smith & Walker, Boston, Mass., at the time of his death. No children.

9. Judson Smith, son of Samuel, grandson of Matthew 6th, b. June 28, 1837, in Middlefield, Mass., m. Aug. 1, 1865, Jerusha Augusta Bushnell, who was b. Feb'y 16, 1843, in Hartford, Ohio.

He pursued his preparatory studies at home and at Williston Seminary. He was an undergraduate in New York Central College from August, 1855, to November, 1857; was tutor in Eleutherian College, Indiana, from November, 1857, to April, 1858; completed the studies of the junior year in Oberlin College, Ohio, and spent the senior year at Amherst College, Massachusetts, where he graduated with the class of 1859. His theological studies were pursued in Union Seminary, New York, and in the department of Theology in Oberlin College, where he graduated with the class of 1863. He was teacher in Monson Academy, Massachusetts, during the year 1861-62, and tutor in Greek and Latin in Oberlin College, Ohio, from 1862-1864; was Professor of Mental and Moral Philosophy in Williston Seminary, Easthampton, Mass., from 1864-1866; Professor in Latin in Oberlin College from 1866-1870; Professor of Church History in Oberlin Theological Seminary from 1870 to 1884; also Lecturer on Modern History in Oberlin College during the same years, from 1870 to 1884; also Lecturer on History at Lake Erie Seminary, Painesville, Ohio, from 1879 to 1884; also President of the Board of Education for the village of Oberlin from 1872 to 1884. In 1884 he removed from Oberlin to Boston (residing three miles from the State House, in that part better known as Roxbury), and became Foreign Secretary of the American Board of Commissioners for Foreign Missions, and holds the same position now, 1890. In October, 1866, he was ordained to the gospel ministry and has preached almost continuously ever since. In 1877 he received the honorary degree of Doctor of Divinity from Amherst College. He was editor of the Bibliotheca Sacra for the year 1883–84, and has been associate editor in the years since.

CHILDREN:

I.—Gertrude Bushnell, b. Mar. 10, 1870. (In 1890 in Wellesley.)
II.—Maurice Billings, b. Nov. 28, 1872. (In 1890 in Harvard.)
III.—Mary Caroline, b. Mar. 2, 1880.
IV.—Margaret Augusta, b. Mar. 2, 1884.

10. Edward Payson Smith, son of Samuel, grandson of Matthew 6th, b. Jan'y 20, 1840, in Middlefield, Mass., m. Nov. 26, 1868, Julia Mack Church, who was b. Nov. 11, 1846, in Middlefield, Mass.

He pursued his academic studies at home, under his brothers and sisters, and in Lewistown Academy, Pennsylvania. He entered Amherst College as Freshman in 1861 and graduated in 1865. He was principal of Hinsdale High school, 1865–67. He pursued the studies of the junior year in Oberlin Theological Seminary with the class of 1869, and the studies of the middle year in Andover Theological Seminary. He was teacher of Greek and Latin for the middle class in Williston Seminary, Easthampton, Mass., 1868–70. He was in Europe for travel and study, 1870–71, and in 1872 returned thither for four months special study in French. He was licensed to preach December, 1871. Since September, 1872, he has been Professor of Modern Languages and Political Science in Worcester Polytechnic Institute, Worcester, Mass., with the exception of one year at Johns Hopkins University, Baltimore, Maryland.

CHILDREN:

I.—Emily Lucy, b. Feb. 10, 1874.
II.—Edward Church, b. Dec. 10, 1877.
III.—Philip Mack, b. Jan. 1, 1883.
IV.—Robert Metcalf, b. Mar. 29, 1886.

Descendants of Jeremiah Smith.

———:o:———

Jeremiah Smith, son of Matthew Smith 5th, gr. son of Matthew 4th, b. June (?) 29, 1758, in E. Haddam, Conn., and d. Dec. 20, 1837. He m. June 17, 1784, Temperance Comstock of Lyme, Conn., who was b. in 1763 and d. Nov. 10, 1843.

CHILDREN:

I.—Jeremiah 2d, b. May 12, 1785.
II.—Azariah, b. Nov. 21, 1786.
III.—Temperance, b. Oct. 27, 1790.
IV.—Sophia, b. May 13, 1793.
V.—Abner C., b. Mar. 29, 1796.
VI.—Erastus, b. April 19, 1799.
VII.—Julia J., b. July 8, 1801.

Descendants of Jeremiah Smith, Jr. or 2d.

———:o:———

Jeremiah Smith 2d, son of Jeremiah, gr. son of Matthew Smith 5th, b. May 12, 1785, and d. Mar. 8, 1864. He m. Nov. 27, 1806, Dorothy Baker, who was b. June 29, 1787, and d. Jan. 16, 1872.

CHILDREN:

I.—Temperance, b. July 15, 1807, d. Jan. 29, 1830.
II.—Jeremiah 3d, b. July 9, 1809.
III.—Dorothy, b. Dec. 3, 1811.
IV.—Henry, b. Sept. 14, 1814.
V.—Gad, b. April 3, 1817.
VI.—Alden, b. July 26, 1819.
VII.—Abner, b. Mar. 22, 1822, d. Oct. 9, 1843.
VIII.—Abby Ann, b. April 28, 1825, d. Dec. 4, 1828.
IX.—Temperance Abby, b. Nov. 29, 1830.

2. Jeremiah Smith 3d, son of Jeremiah 2d, gr. son of Jeremiah (son of Matthew 5th), b. July 9, 1809, and d. April 20, 1887. He m. 1st, April 27, 1837, Margaret S. Robbins, who was b. April 14, 1817, in Woodstown, N. J., and d. April 21, 1857, in Woodstown, N. J. He m. 2d, March, 1861, Mrs. Beulah Davis (*née* Daniels), who was b. ———

CHILDREN: (1st marriage.)

I.—Nathaniel Robbins, b. Jan. 13, 1838.
II.—Harriet Vernon, b. Dec. 19, 1839, d. March, 1849.
III.—Hannah Lawrie, b. May 30, 1841.
IV.—Jeremiah 4th, b. ——— d. ———.

(8)

V.—Jeremiah 5th, b. Feb. 15, 1844.
VI.—Abner Richard, b. June 20, 1846.
VII.—James Lawrie, b. ———, d. in 1853.

Nathaniel R. Smith, son of Jeremiah 3d, gr. son of Jeremiah 2d, b. Jan. 13, 1838, m. March, 1865, Mary Adams.

[Repeated inquiries received no reply.]

CHILDREN:

I.—Margaret Sinclair, b. August, 1865.
II.—Nellie, b. ———.
III.—Carrie, b. October, 1872.

Hannah Lawrie Smith, dau. of Jeremiah 3d, gr. dau. of Jeremiah 2d, b. May 30, 1841, in E. Haddam, Conn., m. April 15, 1872, Wallace Barnes Saterlee, who was b. Jan. 21, 1847, in Plymouth, Conn., and d. Aug. 29, 1884. She is a milliner and resides in Millville, N. J.

CHILDREN:

(All born in Plymouth, Conn.)

I.—Alfred Merritt, b. Sept. 11, 1874.
II.—Wm. Gates, b. May 17, 1877.
III.—Clarence Orville, b. Mar. 27, 1882.

Jeremiah Smith 5th, son of Jeremiah 3d, gr. son of Jeremiah 2d, b. Feb. 15, 1844, in E. Haddam, Conn., m. June 30, 1874, in Essex, Conn., Martha Benton Parker, who was b. Jan. 9, 1855, in Madison, Conn.

CHILDREN:

I.—Horace Parker, b. July 10, 1875, in Woodstown, N. J.
II.—Frank Edward, b. June 29, 1880, in East Hampton, Conn., and d. Aug. 28, 1882, in Chester, Conn.
III.—Charles Henry, b. Dec. 12, 1883, in Chester, Conn.

Abner Richard Smith, son of Jeremiah 3d, gr. son. of Jeremiah 2d, b. June 20, 1846, in E. Haddam, Conn., m. Dec. 8, 1869, Polly Malintha Chapman, who was b. Dec. 14, 1851, in South Glastonbury, Conn.

CHILDREN:

I.—Marinda Lois, b. Mar. 30, 1872.
II.—Bessie Elizabeth, b. Aug. 6, 1874.
III.—Fred Bell, b. July 19, 1876.
IV.—Eugene Lewis, b. Aug. 4, 1878.

3. Dorothy Smith, dau. of Jeremiah Smith 2d, gr. dau. of Jeremiah, b. Dec. 3, 1811, and d. Oct. 25, 1832. She m. Aug. 23, 1831, Elijah Spencer Mack, who was b. May 5, 1809, and d. June 26, 1837.
No children.

4. Henry Smith, son of Jeremiah Smith 2d, gr. son of Jeremiah, b. Sept. 14, 1814, in E. Haddam, Conn., and d. Feb. 19, 1873, in Elizabethport, N. J. He m. Dec. 28, 1853, Mary Eliza-

beth Schenck, who was b. Feb. 4, 1831. He was a physician, and at the time of his marriage was practicing in Neshanic, N. J., where he had an extensive practice and resided many years. His health failing, he purchased a small farm, and soon after, his wife's father dying, she received quite a sum of money. He became quite interested in land in the South and purchased 1,800 acres of cotton land, eight miles from Newbern, N. C., but it proved a poor investment, and he lost all and his wife's money with the rest.

In April, 1871, he moved to Trenton, N. J., and in December to Elizabethport, and they began taking boarders.

After hearing of his mother's death his health failed rapidly and he died in February, 1873, and was buried in Ringoes, N. J.

After his death the children were sent among friends for a time, and then, in 1874, she settled at Lambertville, N. J., and in 1882 removed to Trenton, N. J. She is at present living there. Occupation, a nurse. They had six children.

CHILDREN:

I.—Eliza Schenck Smith, b. Sept. 27, 1854, in Neshanic, N. J., m. April 21, 1874, James Andrew Logan, who was b. Jan. 6, 1853, in Chester, Pa. He is a telegraph operator and they reside in Jersey City, N. J., and have had five children.

CHILDREN:

1. Henry Smith, b. July 29, 1875, at Chester, Pa.
2. Elmer Haverstick, b. Oct. 12, 1876, at Lambertville, N. J., and d. July 29, 1877, at Chester, Pa.
3. John Flinn, b. June 28, 1878, at Jersey City, N. J., and d. there Jan. 31, 1881.
4. Walter Wadsworth, b. Mar. 1, 1882, at Jersey City, N. J., and d. there Mar. 27, 1882.
5. James Wadsworth, b. Jan. 3, 1888, at Jersey City, N. J., and d. there May 5, 1888.

II.—Jeremiah Wadsworth Smith was b. Aug. 3, 1856, in Neshanic, N. J., and d. July 8, 1886. He was a carpenter, a young man of correct habits, a member of the Baptist church, and librarian in S. S. four years previous to his death, which occurred by drowning.

III.—Anna Van Marter Smith was b. May 1, 1859, is by trade a milliner but is out of health and lives with her mother in Trenton, N. J.

IV.—Eveline Cornelia Boyd Smith was b. Nov. 27, 1861, and for over two years has had a situation with the Trenton Watch Co., and resides with her mother in Trenton, N. J.

V.—Nettie Schenck Smith was b. Dec. 5, 1864, and d. Sept. 14, 1883. Was a dressmaker.

VI.—Alleta Van Doren Smith was b. June 21, 1867, and d. Oct. 26, 1869.

5. Gad Smith, son of Jeremiah 2d, gr. son of Jeremiah, b. April 3, 1817, m. 1st, Jan. 27, 1838, Nancy Cone, who was b. in 1814 and d. May —, 1846. He m. 2d, ——————, Mary Elizabeth Bullard, who was b. —————. She lives South.

CHILDREN: (1st marriage.)

I.—Wm. Gad, b. Feb. 14, 1839.
II.—Nancy, d. in infancy.

(2d marriage.)

III.—George Ambrose, b. July 17, 1848.
IV.—Mary Ann Elizabeth, b. Mar. 2, 1850.
V.—Jeremiah J., b. May 8, 1853.

Wm. Gad Smith, son of Gad, gr. son of Jeremiah 2d, b. Feb. 14, 1839, m. Mar. 5, 1868, Elsie Bidwell Williams of Moodus, who was b. Dec. 9, 1849, in Chatham, Conn., and d. Dec. 6, 1885, in Cobalt, Conn., and was buried in Moodus, Conn. He still resides in Cobalt., Conn. He served in the War of the Rebellion.

CHILDREN:

I.—Florence May, b. July 31, 1869, d. April 14, 1880.
II.—Nancy Cone, b. Nov. 2, 1870, d. Aug. 2, 1871.
III.—Henry Floyd, b. Jan. 28, 1872, d. April 22, 1872.
IV.—Marshall Forbes, b. ——————, d.—————.
V.—Wm. Warnock, b. ——————, d. —————.
VI.—Lucy Eveline, b. Feb. 10, 1880, d. July 20, 1880.
VII.—Ida Bella, b. June 15, 1882. After the death of her mother she wished to be called Elsie instead of Ida, so her name was changed to Elsie Bella, and she lives with her father.

Mary A. E. Smith m. Henry S. Haynes. Residence, Meriden, Conn.

6. Alden Smith, son of Jeremiah 2d, gr. son of Jeremiah, b. July 26, 1819, m. 1st, May 2, 1849, Lucinda Ann Purple, who was b. June 16, 1825, and d. April 9, 1861. He m. 2d, June 26, 1867, Harriet Newell Trowbridge, who was b. May 14, 1836, and d. Mar. 3, 1886. He is a man much interested in genealogical works, and particularly in this work, and to him the writer is indebted for much of the history and data of the early settlers. He still resides in E. Haddam, and, until lately, on the old " Smith homestead."

CHILDREN:

(1st marriage.)

I.—Edward Everett, b. Feb. 2, 1850, d. Aug. 9, 1864.
II.—Albert Alden, b. Aug. 11, 1852.
III.—Frederic Wilson, b. Aug. 21, 1854.

(2d marriage.)

IV.—Lucinda Ann, b. July 2, 1868.

Albert Alden Smith, son of Alden, gr. son of Jeremiah 2d, b. Aug. 11, 1852, m. Mar. 2, 1880, Martha Lucy Adams, who was b. Oct. 28, 1857. He d. May 25, 1889. She resides in E. Haddam, Conn.

CHILDREN:

I.—Esther Louisa, b. Dec. 30, 1882.
II.—Edward Everett, b. May 14, 1884.
III.—Bertha Maria, b. Feb. 25, 1887.
IV. —Albert Francis, b. Aug. 8, 1889.

Frederic Wilson Smith, son of Alden, gr. son of Jeremiah 2d, b. Aug. 21, 1854, m. Feb. 29, 1880, Hattie Maria Shailor (dau. of Simon N. Shailor), who was b. Feb. 20, 1859. He d. Dec. 26, 1885. (She m. Henry Cramer and now resides in Colchester, Conn.)

CHILDREN:

I.—Jennie Maria, b. June 2, 1881, d. Jan. 27, 1886.
II.—Alden Nathaniel, b. Jan. 23, 1884, d. Aug. 19, 1884.

Lucinda Ann Smith, dau. of Alden, gr. dau. of Jeremiah 2d, b. July 2, 1868; is unmarried and is at work in a book-bindery in New Haven, Conn.

9. Temperance Abby Smith, dau. of Jeremiah 2d, gr. dau. of Jeremiah, b. Nov. 29, 1830, m. Oct. 31, 1859, William Henry Bennett, who was b. July 10, 1833. They reside in Park Grove cottage, Bridgeport, Conn. They have one child.

CHILDREN:

I.—George Smith Bennett, b. Aug. 4, 1860, m. Jan. 30, 1883, Amy II. Vibert, who was b. June 28, 1865. They reside in Bridgeport and have two children:
 1. Abbie Emma, b. Feb. 17, 1885.
 2. Wm. Henry, b. Oct. 11, 1887.

Descendants of Azariah Smith.

———:o:———

II.

Azariah Smith, son of Jeremiah, gr. son of Matthew Smith 5th, b. Nov. 21, 1786, m. April 27, 1809, Ruthy Ackley, who was b. Jan. 25, 1791, and d. about July 28, 1856. He d. Feb. 12, 1874. He served in the war of 1812, and was always known as "Capt. Smith."

He is said to have left E. Haddam, Conn., in June, 1832, and settled at or near Rome, Ohio, receiving a land warrant.

CHILDREN:

I.—Azariah, b. April 22, 1810.
II.—Ruth, b. Nov. 29, 1811, d. Nov. 1, 1831.
III.—Isaac Ackley, b. May 30, 1814, d. April 8, 1815.
IV.—Isaac Ackley, b. Mar. 23, 1816.
V.—Frederick Burr, b. Oct. 13, 1818.
VI.—Nelson, b. April 24, 1821.
|VII.—Sereno, b. Sept. 13, 1823.
VIII.—Oliver, b. Oct. 20, 1827, d. June 3, 1829.
IX.—Oliver, b. May 23, 1830.
X.—Larissa M., b. Sept. 1, 1832.
XI.—Sophia, b. July 4, 1836.

1. Azariah Smith, son of Azariah, gr. son of Jeremiah (son of Matthew 5th), b. April 22, 1810, in E. Haddam, Conn., and d. Dec. 3, 1881, in Philadelphia, Pa. He m. June 3, 1837, Angeline Steelman, who was b. Mar. 5, 1817, and d. May 20, 1871.

CHILDREN: (all born in Philadelphia, Pa.)

 I.—Hannah Scull, b. Mar. 5, 1838.
 II.—Susanna Scull, b. July 29, 1839.
 III.—Angeline Steelman, b. May 13, 1841.
 IV.—Elizabeth Boyer, b. Jan. 4, 1844; is unmarried and resides in Philadelphia, Pa.
 V.—Edward Leeds, b. April 28, 1847.
 VI.—William Scull, b. June 6, 1849.
 VII.—Rebecca Reeves, } b. May 6, 1853, d. Mar. 16, 1874.
 VIII.—Sarah Braithwaite, } b. May 6, 1853.

I.

Hannah Scull Smith, dau. of Azariah, gr. dau. of Azariah, b. Mar. 5, 1838, m. Sept. 16, 1856, John Dawald, who was b. Feb. 15, 1836. She d. Aug. 4, 1861.

CHILDREN:

 I.—Ida Allelia Angeline, b. June 29, 1857, d. Aug. 19, 1875.
 II.—Ella Alice Alethia, b. Jan. 3, 1859.
 III.—Emma Scull, b. Nov. 30, 1860.

Ella Alice Alethia Dawald, dau. of Hannah Scull, gr. dau. of Azariah, b. Jan. 3, 1859, m. Jan. 20, 1881, Harry Fisher, who was b. Feb. 7, 1856, and they reside in Philadelphia, Pa., and have two children:

 I.—Catharine, b. Jan. 29, 1882.
 II.—Willie, b. Sept. 13, 1883.

Emma Scull Dawald, dau. of Hannah Scull, gr. dau. of Azariah, b. Nov. 30, 1860, m. Feb. 14, 1889, Charles Munch, who was b. Oct. 5, 1861. They reside in Philadelphia, Pa. No children.

II.

Susanna Scull Smith, dau. of Azariah, gr. dau. of Azariah, b. July 29, 1839, m. Aug. 26, 1861, John Michael Voltz, who was b. Oct. 19, 1834. They reside in Philadelphia, Pa.

CHILDREN:

I.—William Takis Lincoln, b. July 24, 1862.
II.—Edward Leeds Smith, b. April 8, 1866, d. Sept. 11, 1867.
III.—Bertha Allelia, b. Feb. 10, 1879.

III.

Angeline Steelman Smith, dau. of Azariah, gr. dau. of Azariah, b. May 13, 1841, and d. Sept. 9, 1886. She m. Jan. 8, 1863, Joseph Dyer Livezey, who was b. Mar. 4, 1840. They had seven children:

I.—Ida Carrie, b. Nov. 24, 1864.
II.—Iola Angeline, b. May 8, 1867.
III.—Azariah Smith, b. Jan. 26, 1869.
IV.—Edward W., b. Dec. 10, 1870.
V.—Jesse Linford, b. May 27, 1875.
VI.—Elmer Bertram, b. Aug. 1, 1877.
VII.—Ella Maud, b. Sept. 14, 1880, d. April 10, 1881.

Ida Carrie Livezey, dau. of Angeline Steelman, gr. dau. of Azariah, b. Nov. 24, 1864, m. Aug. 25, 1884, George Washington Jackson, who was b. April 15, 1862. They reside in Philadelphia, Pa.

CHILDREN:

I.—John S., b. June 4, 1885, d. April 16, 1888.

Iola Angeline Livezey, dau. of Angeline Steelman, gr. dau. of Azariah, b. May 8, 1867, m. May 27, 1889, William King, who was b. Feb. 6, 1868. They reside in Philadelphia, Pa. No children.

V.

Edward Leeds Smith, son of Azariah, gr. son of Azariah, b. April 28, 1847, m. 1st, Oct. 10, 1871, Lydia Ann Heller, who was b. Sept. 11, 1845, and d. Nov. 17, 1879. He m. 2d, Aug. 22, 1886, Katie Fratts, who was b. June 10, 1856, in Philadelphia, Pa., where they now reside.

CHILDREN:

(2d marriage.)

I.—Edward Steelman, b. June 3, 1887.

VI.

Wm. Scull Smith, son of Azariah, gr. son of Azariah, b. June 6, 1849, m. Oct. 15, 1878, Ellen Boyer Dubree, who was b. May 19, 1849, in Pottstown, Pa. They reside in Philadelphia, Pa.

CHILDREN:

I.—Eva Scull, b. April 2, 1880.
II.—Sallie Steelman, b. April 9, 1882.
III.—Wm. Scull, b. Sept. 9, 1885.

VIII.

Sarah Braithwaite Smith, dau. of Azariah, gr. dau. of Azariah, b. May 6, 1853, m. Jan. 3, 1884, Charles Henry Walker, who was b. July 4, 1854. They reside in Philadelphia, Pa. No children.

4. Isaac Ackley Smith, son of Azariah, gr. son of Jeremiah, b. Mar. 23, 1816, m. Mar. 11, 1855, Tamson Beckett Newkirk, who was b. Dec. 19, 1834. They reside in Salem, N. J.

CHILDREN:

I.—Ella Virginia, b. July 30, 1856.
II.—Ida Lenora, b. Nov. 21, 1859, d. Nov. 26, 1862.
III.—Jennie Newkirk, b. Sept. 13, 1862, d. Dec. 25, 1863.
IV.—Lillie Bell, b. April 18, 1867.
V.—Frank Reed, b. Jan. 22, 1876.

Ella Virginia Smith, dau. of Isaac Ackley, gr. dau. of Azariah, b. July 30, 1856, m. Nov. 10, 1875, John Davison Cawley, who was b. Dec. 10, 1855. They reside in Wilmington, Del.

CHILDREN:

I.—Jennie Newkirk, b. June 21, 1877.
II.—Bertha, b. Sept. 27, 1879.
III.—William, b. Nov. 22, 1882.

5. Frederick Burr Smith, son of Azariah, gr. son of Jeremiah, b. Oct. 13, 1818, m. 1st, May 18, 1845, Catharine Lucinda Crowell, who was b. April 26, 1825, in Rome, Ohio, and d. July 16, 1846. He m. 2d, Dec. 17, 1846, Artemisia Leonora Foote, who was b. April 30, 1825, in Morgan, Ohio, and d. Sept. 12, 1881. He now resides in Eagleville, Ohio.

CHILDREN: (2d marriage.)

I.—Florence Agnes, b. June 9, 1849. She m. Dec. 25, 1871, James Archibald, who was b. Nov. 21, 1847, in Coitsville, Ohio. She d. May 8, 1883, leaving five children.

CHILDREN:

I.—Forrester Ray, b. Dec. 4, 1873.
II.—Fred., b. Nov. 2, 1876.
III.—Arthur, b. Oct. 26, 1879.
IV.—Bessie, b. Feb. 13, 1881, d. Sept. 26, 1887.
V.—Lee, b. Mar. 16, 1883.

6. Nelson Smith, son of Azariah Smith, gr. son of Jeremiah, b. April 24, 1821, m. Sept. 2, 1843, Mary Merritt, who was b. April 19, 1821. Their present address is New Lyme Station, Ohio. No children.

7. Sereno Smith, son of Azariah Smith, gr. son of Jeremiah, b. Sept. 13, 1823, m. Mar. or May 30, 1848, Mary Phelps, who was b. Nov. 7, 1828, in Williamsfield, Ohio, and d. Oct. 25, 1889, in Kingsville, Ohio. They resided in Rome, Ohio, where he was murdered, and in the Ashtabula Sentinel was the following account:

"Sereno Smith was a well-to-do farmer, forty-eight years of age, unassuming and universally respected in the locality in which he lived. On the morning of April 25, 1872, he mysteriously disappeared from his home, and it was thought by his family and friends that he had, in a fit of mental aberration, wandered away or committed suicide, although no cause could be assigned for such an act. With this impression, woods were searched, streams and ponds were dragged with no result.

"About two weeks after the disappearance of Mr. Smith, Mr. J. H. Phelps, brother of Mrs. Smith, came to Rome, and, while sleeping, dreamed that his brother-in-law had been murdered and the body concealed in a large manure heap near the barn. Not being a firm believer in dreams he deemed it more a fallacy than a reality. Still being so strongly impressed and the search being still continued, on Sunday morning, May 12, a search was made at the place indicated in the dream, when the body was soon found, presenting a horrid sight and revealing a most brutal murder. The skull was beaten in as by an ax. Suspicion at once pointed to one John Housel, a young man who had been for the past year in the employ of Mr. Smith, and the chain of circumstantial evidence is so strong that he probably will pay the penalty of the crime. As there was no conceivable motive for the murder, the deed was as mysterious as it was brutal."

Since the above was written Housel has made a full confession of his crime and is now serving a life sentence in the Ohio penitentiary.

Sereno lived as neighbor to his brother Nelson, and the house has been unoccupied since—for seventeen years it has been vacant.

They had no children.

9. Oliver Smith, son of Azariah, gr. son of Jeremiah, b. May 23, 1830, m. Aug. 31, 1856, Mary Oriette Crosby, who was b. Aug. 5, 1836, and educated at Grand River Institute, Austinburg, Ohio. They reside now in Dorset, Ohio. He owns mills there and at Jefferson, and consider their home in Ashtabula, though they do not remain there all the time. He was the seventh son in succession, and has been commonly called "Doctor" or "Doc" by his intimate friends.

He received a common school education with one or two years at the academy at Kingsville, Ohio.

At the age of seventeen he went to Philadelphia, and there engaged in same business in which his older brothers were interested, but returned home in a few years and went into the lumber business, and for thirty years was a manufacturer and an extensive dealer in lumber and owner of many mills in Ashtabula Co., Ohio.

CHILDREN:

I.—Oliver Conrad, b. July 31, 1857, and at the age of eleven was crippled for life, but is now able to work a little on the farm. Was educated at Grand River Institute.

II.—Mabel Oriette, b. May 11, 1868, educated at Grand River Institute, where she graduated, taught a year and has completed one year in a medical course at Cleveland, O. The whole family are members of Trinity church (Episcopal), Jefferson, Ohio.

10. Larissa M. Smith, dau. of Azariah, gr. dau. of Jeremiah, b. Sept. 1, 1832, in Rome, Ohio, m. Nov. 7, 1850, Marquis Lafayette Strickland, who was b. Nov. 22, 1829, in New Lyme, Ohio. She d. July 16, 1882. He resides in Dodgeville, O.

CHILDREN:

I.—Edna Luella, b. Jan. 22, 1871.

11. Sophia Smith, dau. of Azariah, gr. dau. of Jeremiah, b. July 4, 1836, in E. Haddam, Conn., m. Dec. 31, 1854, Ashbel Clark Baldwin, who was b. Dec. 3, 1830, in Deep River, Conn.

They reside in Cincinnati, O., he being a member of the firm of McFarlan, Baldwin & Co., wholesale grocers and general commission merchants.

CHILDREN:

I.—Forrester Beaumont, b. Oct. 21, 1855.

Forrester B. Baldwin, son of Sophia, gr. son of Azariah, was b. Oct. 21, 1855, in Rome, Ohio, m. Sept. 15, 1881, Ida Kemp Cheeseman, who was b. Sept. 28, 1861, in Cincinnati, O. They reside in Cincinnati.

CHILDREN:

I.—Ashbel William, b. May 18, 1884.
II.—Ralph Arthur, b. Aug. 1, 1886.

Descendants of Temperance Smith.

---:o:---

III.

Temperance Smith, dau. of Jeremiah, gr. dau. of Matthew Smith 5th, b. Oct. 27, 1790, m. Oct. 27, 1805, Joseph Osborn Ackley, who was b. ———— ————, and d. July ——, 1818. She d. Feb. 29, 1812, leaving two children. He m. again the following September. He was lieutenant in the war of 1812. He removed from E. Haddam, Conn., to Weston, N. Y., and was killed at the raising of the famous Carthage bridge (being master builder of the bridge), by the falling of the derrick. He endeavored to avoid its fall by running, but fell himself and the timber fell upon his head, sinking it some inches into the ground, leaving its shape there, where it remained some weeks afterward.

CHILDREN : (1st marriage.)

I.—Eveline Cornelia, b. Aug. 3, 1808.
II.—Sophia Smith, b. May 27, 1810, d. Mar. 5, 1819.

1. Eveline Cornelia Ackley, dau. of Temperance, gr. dau. of Jeremiah, b. Aug. 3, 1808, m. April 17, 1827, William Bradbury Boyd, who was b. Sept. 25, 1800, and d. July 14, 1883. She d. Feb. 8, 1868.

CHILDREN :

I.—Elizabeth, b. June, 1827, d. September, 1827.
II.—Eveline Cornelia, b. Aug. 22, 1829, d. May 7, 1836

III.—Ellen Sophia, b. April 21, 1833.
IV.—Sarah Jane, b. Dec. 22, 1834.
V.—Wm. Bradbury, b. Sept. 25, 1839, d. in 1840.
VI.—Frederic Ackley, b. Sept. 17, 1841, d. in 1842.
VII.—Isabel Walker, b. Nov. 12, 1843.
VIII.—Frederic Wm. Osborn, b. October, 1848, d. in 1849.

Ellen Sophia Boyd, dau. of Eveline Cornelia, gr. dau. of Temperance, b. April 21, 1833, m. Dec. 2, 1857, Charles A. Fiske, who was b. Mar. 7, 1816, in Medfield, Mass., and d. May 1, 1879. She resides in Cambridge, Mass.

CHILDREN:

I.—Wm. Boyd, b. Nov. 17, 1858.
II.—Cornelia, b. Nov. 1, 1861.

They both reside in Cambridge, Mass., and Wm. Boyd Fiske is a physician.

Sarah Jane Boyd, dau. of Eveline Cornelia, gr. dau. of Temperance, b. Dec. 22, 1834, m. 1st, July 13, 1864, Erastus H. Tyler, who was b. Dec. 5, 1835, and d. Dec. 9, 1881, in Medway, Mass. She m. 2d, Dec. 27, 1883, Benjamin Glidden, who was b. Feb. 25, 1839. She d. May 11, 1887.

CHILDREN:

(1st marriage.)

I.—Eveline Harding, b. Sept. 2, 1868.
She resides in Beverly, Mass.

Isabel Walker Boyd, dau. of Eveline Cornelia, gr. dau. of Temperance, b. Nov. 12, 1843, m. Feb. 22, 1872, Wm. Brown Roberts, who was b. Jan. 22, 1847, in Fair Haven, Mass. They now reside in Medfield, Mass.

CHILDREN.

I.—Joseph Arthur, b. Dec. 1, 1873.
II.—George Herbert, b. May 7, 1876.
III.—Ellen Boyd, b. June 8, 1878.

Descendants of Sophia Smith.

——:o:——

IV.

Sophia Smith, dau. of Jeremiah, gr. dau. of Matthew 5th, b. May 13, 1793, m. Feb. 13, 1812, Joseph Brainard, who was b. Mar. 5, 1786, and d. Dec. 8, 1843, and was buried in Philadelphia. She d. in E. Haddam, Nov. 19, 1845, and was buried there in Mount Parnassus cemetery. No children.

Descendants of Abner Comstock Smith.

——:o:——

V.

Abner Comstock Smith, son of Jeremiah, gr. son of Matthew 5th, b. Mar. 29. 1796, m. 1st, May 25, 1820, Electa Warner, who was b. Jan. 23, 1798 and d. April 24, 1824. He m. 2d, April 1, 1826, Hope Marshall, who was b. May 11, 1805 or 1806, and d. Aug. 26, 1883. He d. Mar. 5, 1876, and both were buried in cemetery at Mount Parnassus.

CHILDREN : (2d marriage.)

I.—Charles Belden, b. July 11, 1827.
II.—Benjamin Marshall, b. Aug. 24, 1829.
III.—Louisa, b. Aug. 9, 1831.
IV.—Nancy Almira, b. April 8, 1834.
V.—Temperance Comstock, b. Jan. 10, 1837, d. Sept. 25, 1840.
VI.—Maria Elizabeth, b. Sept. 24, 1839, d. Dec. 16, 1865.
VII.—Candace Comstock, b. Oct. 3, 1841, d. Mar. 9, 1857.
VIII.—Julia Sophia, b. Jan. 29, 1844, d. Aug. 19, 1866.
IX.—Abner Comstock, b. Oct. 30, 1846.
X.—Robbins Tracy, b. Aug. 5, 1849.

1. Charles Belden Smith, son of Abner Comstock, gr. son of Jeremiah, b. July 11, 1827, m. Mar. 18, 1863, Julia Brown Ford, who was b. Aug. 29, 1837, and d. Feb. 24, 1875. He resides in E. Haddam, Conn. No children.

2. Benjamin Marshall Smith, son of Abner Comstock, gr. son of Jeremiah, b. Aug. 24, 1829, m. June 1, 1864, Virginia Donelly (usually called Jennie), who was b. July 19, 1842. He d. Mar. 9, 1868, and his widow resides with her children in Philadelphia, Pa.

CHILDREN:

I.—Joseph A., b. Feb. 13, 1865.
II.—Marie E., b. Jan. 23, 1867.

Joseph A. is married but get no answer to letters.

3. Louisa Smith, dau. of Abner C., gr. dau. of Jeremiah, b. Aug. 9, 1831, m. Mar. 31, 1858, John Chamberlain Gibbs, who was b. Jan. 12, 1836. They reside in Brookfield, Mass., and have no children.

4. Nancy Almira Smith, dau. of Abner C., gr. dau. of Jeremiah, b. April 8, 1834, m. June 18, 1856, Henry M. Moulton, who was b. June 18, 1836. They reside in East Haddam, Conn.

CHILDREN:

I.—Charles Edward, b. Mar. 3, 1863, d. Sept. 3, 1865.
II.—Ellen Louisa, b. June 28, 1865.

9. Abner Comstock Smith, son of Abner Comstock, gr. son of Jeremiah, b. Oct. 30, 1846, m. Nov. 24, 1870, Elizabeth Jacobs, who was b. Sept. 17, 1848. They reside in E. Haddam, Conn.

CHILDREN:

I.—Eveline Cornelia, b. Sept. 30, 1871.
II.—Clara Isabella, b. Aug. 26, 1874.
III.—Walter Marshall, b. Sept. 6, 1876, d. July 31, 1878.
IV.—George Clarence, b. Sept. 15, 1882.
V.—Robert Marshall, b. Dec. 17, 1887.

10. Robbins Tracy Smith, son of Abner Comstock, gr. son of Jeremiah, b. Aug 5, 1849, m. Nov. 1, 1875, Catharine Smith Sneyd, who was b. Mar. 8, 1856. He d. Feb. 5, 1884, and his widow resides in E. Haddam, Conn.

CHILDREN:

I.—Adelaide Fontaine, b. Aug. 20, 1876.
II.—Josephine Perkenpine, b. July 15, 1878.
III.—Charles Abner, b. Nov. 7, 1881.
IV.—Robbins Tracy, b. Sept 2, 1883, d. June 8, 1884.

Descendants of Erastus Smith.

VI.

Erastus Smith, son of Jeremiah, gr. son of Matthew 5th, b. April 19, 1799, m. June 4, 1818, Nancy Allen, who was b. Oct. 14, 1795, and d. July 4, 1845, in Philadelphia, Pa., and was buried there. He is now living with his son in East Haddam, Conn., the only one of that generation living, including those connected with the different families by marriage; the only descendant born before 1800 now living.

CHILDREN:

I.—William Erastus, b. Feb. 18, 1819.
II.—Eveline Cornelia, b. June 6, 1826.

1. William Erastus Smith, son of Erastus, gr. son of Jeremiah, b. Feb. 18, 1819, m. Aug. 3, 1845, Catharine Perkenpine, who was b. July 10, 1823. They reside in E. Haddam, Conn. No children.

2. Eveline Cornelia Smith, dau. of Erastus, gr. dau. of Jeremiah, b. June 6, 1826, m. Aug. 19, 1846, William Henry Tracy, who was b. April 28, 1827. She d. Jan. 16, 1860. No children.

Descendants of Julia Jennings Smith.

VII.

Julia Jennings Smith, dau. of Jeremiah, gr. dau. of Matthew 5th, b. July 8, 1801, and d. Aug. 6, 1889. She m. Oct. 8, 1818, Christopher Columbus Gates, who was b. July 29, 1793, and d. June 1, 1880. They resided in E. Haddam, Conn.

CHILDREN:

I.—Edward Timothy, b. Oct. 8, 1819.
II.—Julia Sophia, b. Aug. 28, 1821.
III.—Joseph Brainard, b. Oct. 16, 1823, d. Jan. 17, 1844, of consumption.
IV.—George Gleason, b. Dec. 25, 1825.
V.—James Percival, b. Dec. 8, 1827.
VI.—Wm. Richard, b. July 1, 1831.
VII.—Emma Maria, b. July 4, 1836; unmarried and resides at E. Haddam, Conn., during the summer, and in Malden, Mass., in the winter.
VIII.—Francis Alonzo, b. Sept. 16, 1838.
IX.—Charles Comstock, b. April 22, 1842, d. December 24, 1861, of consumption.
X.—Henry Irvin, b. Mar. 2, 1847, d. Jan. 9, 1863, of consumption.

1. Edward Timothy Gates, son of Julia J., gr. son of Jeremiah, b. Oct 8, 1819, m. May 2, 1843, Sarah Elizabeth Cook, who was b. June 25, 1821, in E. Haddam, Conn. They reside in Thomaston, Conn.

CHILDREN:

I.—Wm. Cook, b. Mar. 29, 1844.
II.—Charles Christopher, b. May 5, 1846.
III.—Adaline Elizabeth, b. Dec. 23, 1849, d. Aug. 3, 1877.
IV.—Edward Henry, b. Jan. 13, 1857.

Wm. Cook Gates, son of Edward Timothy, gr. son of Julia J., b. Mar. 29, 1844, m. Nov. 21, 1867, Mrs. Adaline S. Mixter (*née* Barton), who was b. Mar. 29, 1840. They reside in South Hadley Falls, Mass.
No children.

Charles Christopher Gates, son of Edward T., gr. son of Julia J., b. May 5, 1846, m. Annie Steele, and they have four children, one boy and three girls. [Repeated letters to him and to his father receive no further information.] His address is Ansonia, Conn.

Edward Henry Gates, son of Edward T., gr. son of Julia J., b. Jan. 13, 1857, m. Nov. 23, 1879, Anna Berthold, who was b. July 5, 1853. He is in a store in Hartford, Conn., his family living at Thomaston, Conn.

CHILDREN:

I.—Frederick Wm. Berthold, b. Sept. 6, 1881.
II.—Lizzie Pauline, b. Mar. 12, 1888.

2. Julia Sophia Gates, dau. of Julia J., gr. dau. of Jeremiah, b. Aug. 28, 1821, m. Aug. 27, 1850, Asa Strong Kelsey, who was b. June 15, 1823, in Southbury, Conn. They reside in Plymouth, Conn.

CHILDREN:

I.—Julia Sarah, b. June 26, 1856.
II.—Emma Sophia, b. Feb. 3, 1858; unmarried.
III.—Frank Gates, b. Jan. 11, 1861.
IV.—Joseph Strong, b. Dec. 27, 1863, d. July 6, 1871.

Julia Sarah Kelsey, dau. of Julia Sophia, gr. dau. of Julia J., b. June 26, 1856, m. Dec. 13, 1877, Marshall Wells Leach, who was b. Feb. 17, 1854, in Torrington, Conn.

CHILDREN:

I.—Lawrence Luther, b. Dec. 30, 1878.
II.—Elsie Sophia, b. Aug. 10, 1881.
III.—Margaret Kelsey, b. Sept. 10, 1887.

Frank Gates Kelsey, son of Julia Sophia, gr. son of Julia J., b. Jan. 11, 1861, m. Jan. 5, 1887, Louise Jenkins Kitson, who was b. June 16, 1862, in Morrisville, Pa., and d. Feb. 5, 1888. No children.

4. George Gleason Gates, son of Julia J., gr. son of Jeremiah, b. Dec. 25, 1825, at Moodus, Conn., m., at New London, Conn., July 16, 1848, Charlotte Renouf Ewen, who was b. Dec.

10, 1830, in New London, Conn. He was a shoemaker and d. July 1, 1887, of erysipelas, in Hartford, Conn.

CHILDREN:

I.—Georgie, b. April 29, 1849, in Moodus, Conn., m., at Hartford, Conn., Mar. 9, 1875, Louis Brush, a printer, who was b. April 11, 1842, in Buffalo, N. Y. They reside in Buffalo, N. Y.

CHILDREN:

I.—Lottie Margaret, b. Nov. 29, 1877, in Hartford, Conn.
II.—Hazel Belle, b. April 8, 1885, in Manchester, Conn.

5. James Percival Gates, son of Julia J., gr. son of Jeremiah, b. Dec. 8, 1827, m. June 6, 1847, Ellen Carrier, who was b. July 8, 1830, in Westchester, Conn., and d. Sept. 27, 1873. He d. Nov. 4, 1855, of consumption.

CHILDREN:

I.—Frances Ellen, b. Mar. 8, 1849.
II.—Catharine Cornelia, b. Sept. 7, 1851.
III.—Frederic, b. —————————, d. in infancy.

Frances Ellen Gates, dau. of James Percival, gr. dau. of Julia J., b. Mar. 8, 1849, m. 1st, Aug. 28, 1867, Howard Ackley, who was b. Mar. 2, 1848, and d. Nov. 25, 1879. She m. 2d, ——————, Arthur Cooper, who was b. ——————. They reside in New York city.

CHILDREN: (1st marriage.)

I.—Wallace Howard, b. Aug. 1, 1870, d. Aug. 1, 1872.

The above family are in South America, so that nothing further could be ascertained.

Catharine Cornelia Gates, dau. of James Percival, gr. dau. of Julia J., b. Sept. 7, 1851, m. May 23, 1874, George Ackley (brother of Howard Ackley), who was b. Oct. 1, 1853. They reside in East Hampton, Conn.

CHILDREN:

I.—Howard Preston, b. July 18, 1876, d. April 30, 1890.
II.—Ellen Lydia, b. Oct. 14, 1878, d. Aug. 16, 1879.
III.—Edwin Chauncy, b. July 28, 1880.

6. Wm. Richard Gates, son of Julia J., gr. son of Jeremiah, b. July 1, 1831, and d. Aug. 21, 1856, of consumption. He m. June 12, 1853, Adelaide Witherell, who was b. May 25, 1832, in Portland, Conn. She now resides in Hillhouse, Lake Co., Ohio. No children.

8. Francis Alonzo Gates, son of Julia J., gr. son of Jeremiah, b. Sept. 16, 1838, m. Jan. 1, 1867, Sarah Teressa Garlock, who was b. Feb. 3, 1844. They reside in Bristol, Conn.

CHILDREN:

I.—Josephine Clare, b. June 23, 1868.
II.—George Walton, b. June 18, 1870.
III.—Charles Weston, b. June 22, 1875.

(11)

Descendants of Calvin Smith.

———:o:———

Calvin Smith, son of Matthew 5th, gr. son of Matthew 4th, b. Nov. 28, 1760, in E. Haddam, Conn., m. Jan. 15, 1784, Anna Anable, who was b. October, 1762, in E. Haddam, Conn. (She was a sister of Asenath Anable, who married Calvin's brother, Matthew.) She d. July 29, 1852, in Middlefield, Mass. He d. Nov. 18, 1832, in Middlefield, Mass. Just what year he removed his family to Middlefield is not certain, but the first child born there was in 1790. It is supposed that he came in 1783, with his brother Matthew, and both purchased farms, Matthew's being now owned by John Metcalf Smith, and Calvin's by George W. Cottrell.

CHILDREN:

I.—Calvin, b. July 9, 1784, in E. Haddam, Conn., and d. Sept. 10, 1810.

II.—Betsey, b. Jan. 27, 1786, in E. Haddam, Conn.

III.—Asa, b. Mar. 23, 1788, in E. Haddam, Conn.

The remaining children b. in Middlefield, Mass.

IV.—Anna, b. April 10, 1790.

V.—Orrin, b. Dec. 31, 1791.

VI.—Oliver, b. Oct. 28, 1793.

VII.—Ambrose, b. June 17, 1796.

VIII.—Obadiah, b. May 20, 1798.

IX.—Sally, b. Feb. 15, 1800.

X.—Sylvester, b. Mar. 25, 1802, d. Aug. 14, 1810.

XI.—Ebenezer, b. Aug. 10, 1804.

XII.—Temperance, b. June 19, 1807, d. Aug. 17, 1810.

Descendants of Betsey Smith.

---:o:---

II.

Betsey Smith, dau. of Calvin, gr. dau. of Matthew 5th, b. January 26, 1786, in E. Haddam, Conn., m. Mar. 3, 1806, William Ingham, who was b. Feb. 21, 1782, in Middlefield, Mass., and died Dec. 1, 1832, in Cato, N. Y. She d. July 16, 1826, in Cato, N. Y.

Mr. Ingham in early life was a merchant, and was postmaster at Cato, now Meridian, N. Y., for twenty years. He was thrice married, Betsey being his first wife.

CHILDREN:

I.—William Smith, b. Aug. 4, 1807.
II.—Samuel, b. Feb. 9, 1809, d. Mar. 30, 1809.
III.—Betsey, b. Jan. 15, 1810, d. Jan. 17, 1810.
IV.—Betsey Maria, b. June 21, 1811.
V.—Maria, b. June 21, 1813, d. Aug. 2, 1813.
VI.—Alzina Anna, b. April 22, 1822.
VII.—Albert Hoyt, b. Feb. 13, 1824, d. July 25, 1827.

1. William Smith Ingham, son of Betsey, gr. son of Calvin, b. Aug. 4, 1807, in Middlefield, Mass., m. 1st, Oct. 30, 1828, Huldah Bacon (dau. of Rev. Elijah Bacon of Ira, N. Y.), who was b. June 26, 1810, and d. Aug. 25, 1854, in Meridian, N. Y. He m. 2d, Nov. 18, 1854, Mrs. Maria Houston (*née* Reed), who was b. Feb. 27, 1816, and d. Jan. 31, 1869. (No children.) He

d. June 3, 1867. He was at one time postmaster and merchant at Cato, N. Y. He instituted and carried on several kinds of business, and gave employment to many men and women. Failing in business about 1857, he moved to Hannibal, Missouri, where he was appointed collector of internal revenue, under the administration of President Lincoln ; afterwards he was mayor of the city, and at the time of his death was serving his third term. He took an active part in religious matters.

CHILDREN : (1st marriage.)

I.—Fernando Hargrave, b. Nov. 2, 1829, and d. Jan. 3, 1853. (A young man of much promise.)

II.—Maladine Huldah, b. Jan. 21, 1834.

III.—Ianthe Iphigene, b. May 15, 1839. She grew to be a beautiful and accomplished young lady, and d. Jan. 7, 1859, in Hannibal, Mo.

IV.—William Bacon, b. Mar. 29, 1852.

Maladine Huldah Ingham, dau. of Wm. Smith, gr. dau. of Betsey, b. Jan. 21, 1834, m. 1st, Oct. 11, 1848, Samuel A. Goodyear, who was b. Jan. 29, 1826, in Genoa, N. Y., and d. June 3, 1850, in Meridian, N. Y. She m. 2d, Aug. 4, 1852, David W. Emerick, who was b. Feb. 14, 1826, in Meridian, N. Y., and d. Dec. 6, 1864, in Fulton, N. Y. She m. 3d, the latter part of 1865, Dorastses Kellogg, who was b. Jan. 10, 1808, in Skaneateles, N. Y., and d. at Oswego Falls, N. Y., Feb. 1, 1885. She d. at the home of her daughter in Beatrice, Neb., Feb, 14, 1885.

CHILDREN :

(1st marriage.)

I.—Ernastine Hermenia, b. Oct. 19, 1849, in Meridian, N. Y., and d. there, June 27, 1852.

(2d marriage.)

II.—Nellie, b. Jan. 26, 1862, m. Nov. 22, 1877, Fred M. Case, who was b. Oct. 9, 1840, in New York city. He is a photographer, and they reside in Beatrice, Neb.

CHILDREN:

I.—Harry Ingham, b. Sept. 10, 1883.

William Bacon Ingham, son of William Smith, gr. son of Betsey, b. Mar. 29, 1852, m. April 12, 1875, Eulalie R. Hurt (dau. of Floyd and Clara Hurt), who was b. April 7, 1855.

After the death of his father he removed with his step-mother to New York, and was placed in the Preparatory Military Academy at Sing Sing, Rev. David Holbrook, Principal. After living in Fulton, N. Y., a short time, he removed to Saltville, Va., where he was employed, for seven or more years, as bookkeeper for "The Holston Salt and Plaster Co.," and in 1880 removed to Abingdon, Va., where he is at present, engaged in the manufacture of plug tobacco.

CHILDREN:

I.—Floyd Fulkerson, b. Aug. 18, 1878, d. Nov. 25, 1883.
II.—Wm. Smith, b. May 31, 1880, d. Feb. 17, 1881.
III.—Samuel Ellis, b. Aug. 12, 1885, d. Oct. 13, 1885.
IV.—Ralph Erving, b. June 9, 1887.
V.—George Reed, b. Feb. 28, 1889.

4. Betsey Maria Ingham, dau. of Betsey, gr. dau. of Calvin, b. June 21, 1811, in Pittsfield, Mass., m. Jan. 8, 1827, John Hall Dudley, then a school teacher and an infidel, but at the age of twenty-seven he was converted and was an honored and useful minister of the gospel. He was pastor of several churches in Central New York, but in 1844 moved to Delavan, Wis., and was the second pastor of the First Baptist church for five and one-half years, then pastor of Sugar Creek fourteen years; after that at East Delavan. He was one of the most prominent Abolitionists of his day and a man of strong convictions and set principles, and his influence was felt in the community where he lived. He was b. Sept. 7, 1803, in Andover, Vt. (son of Jonathan and Sophia Dudley), and from 1844 until his death made Delavan, Wis., his home. He d. Feb. 7, 1868. His widow d. Aug. 11, 1868, at Delavan, Wisconsin. They had five children.

CHILDREN:

I.—Arvilla Maria, b. Oct. 19, 1827; unmarried and an invalid.

II.—William Henry, b. Sept. 22, 1829.

III.—Carroll Edgar Ingham, b. April 18, 1835. He was a delicate child and was taken, in 1852, to New Mexico by his uncle, Rev. H. W. Read, and in that fine climate became healthy. Mr. Read taught him the Spanish language, and he was translator for the mission, and after the church at Albuquerque was established he was clerk and also licensed to preach. In 1854 he returned to Madison University, Hamilton, N. Y., to complete his studies. He became teacher of the Spanish language in the University and in the Ladies' Academy in the village. Rev. Eaton, the president of the University, said: "Carroll Dudley was one of the smartest and best students that ever studied there." His death occurred there (by drowning) July 10, 1858.

IV.—John Arthur, b. Mar. 28, 1845, d. Nov. 14, 1845.

V.—Helen Alzina, b. Mar. 4, 1847.

Wm. Henry Dudley, son of Betsey Maria, gr. son of Betsey, b. Sept. 22, 1829, m. Feb. 28, 1856, Sarah J. Taylor, who was b. July 31, 1832. He spent some four years in California and Nevada, leaving his wife and two sons with his parents. After he returned he was in New York city, selling mining properties. He d. there March 27, 1869, his wife, with her two boys, returning to her friends in Ohio. They had three children. She now resides at Lake Geneva, Wis.

CHILDREN:

I.—Charles Carroll, b. Jan. 27, 1857, at Delavan, Wis.; unmarried and resides at Lake Geneva, Wis.
II.—Arthur John, b. Jan. 29, 1859, at Delavan, Wis.
III.—Mary Ellen, b. April 24, 1869, at Crystal Lake, Ill., and resides with her mother.

Arthur John Dudley, son of Wm. Henry, gr. son of Betsey Maria, b. Jan. 29, 1859, at Delavan, Wis., m. Oct. 31, 1883, Lora Mary Wylie, who was b. April 21, 1862, at Lafayette, Wis. He d. Mar. 4, 1890. The "Lake Geneva News" contained the following: "Mr. Arthur J. Dudley, a valued employé of Lyon & Healy, died at his home, Lake Geneva, Wis., on the 4th inst., of typhoid fever, after an illness of five weeks. The deceased had a bright future before him in his chosen vocation, as he displayed business abilities of high order and joined to this had a genial, attractive manner which endeared him to all with whom he came in contact. He was a man of high moral character, and his untimely death will be regretted by all who knew him. He left a wife and one child, who will have sincere condolence of his employers, his fellow-workers and a wide circle of personal and business friends."

CHILDREN:

I.—Carroll Arthur, b. Sept. 26, 1885.
II.—Daughter, b. Nov. 27, 1887, d. Jan. 20, 1888.

Helen Alziná Dudley, dau. of Betsey Maria, gr. dau. of Betsey, b. Mar. 4, 1847, m. Nov. 1. 1864, David M. Bennett, who was b. Aug. 2, 1816, at Laurens, N. Y., and d. April 16, 1879, at Napiersville, Ill. She now resides in Elgin, Ill.

CHILDREN:

I.—Gladys Gustine, b. Mar. 24, 1867, at Delavan, Wis., and d. Feb. 5, 1886, at Lake Geneva, Wis.

6. Alzina Anna, dau. of Wm. Ingham and Betsey Smith, was b. April 22, 1822, m. June 13, 1844, Rev. H. W. Read, who was b. July 17, 1819, in Connecticut.

She was said to be one of the best English grammarians in New York State when but eighteen years of age. Her talents, says a friend, were of an unusually high order and her attainments numerous and superior. She studied and taught several languages, vocal and instrumental music, and when she had the prospect of becoming a minister's wife, she took a course of studies in theology. At eighteen years of age she was secretary of "The Female Moral Reform Society." Her reports were models of penmanship, grammatical accuracy, charming composition, terse, chaste, yet vigorous and elegant documents.

She had then and for many years after acquaintances and correspondents, such as Mrs. Sarah J. Hale, Mrs. M. G. Clark, Grace Greenwood, Maria Hall, Mrs. Fales, Mrs. Emily B. Judson and many others.

[Perhaps it will be well here to give a little personal history of H. W. Read before giving an account of their missionary life.]

He was born of good Revolutionary (War) Baptists, in Jewett City, Conn. His father and grandfather were both born there, both Baptist ministers and preached about forty years each. His father moved to Central New York when he was but two years of age. At six years of age he signed the temperance pledge, and has faithfully kept it to this day, and has never used tobacco in any form. At ten years of age he was converted and at once began holding meetings with the children of the neighborhood. In 1838 he attended Rev. Wright's academy in Oswego, and was baptized in the Oswego river, by Rev. Wm. Hutchins. In 1840 was licensed and commenced preaching. In the spring of 1841 entered Madison University at Hamilton, N. Y., and was at once appointed bookkeeper for the Education Society. Had a large S. S. four miles away, preached during term time, and held protracted meetings during vacation.

A few months before he was ready to graduate in his classical, theological and medical studies, Alzina, then his fiancée, was sick almost unto death, so that her physician and a large council of eminent physicians, after a most careful and thorough investigation and diagnosis of her case, reluctantly but unanimously decided that there was no possibility of her recovery and that she could not live more than twelve weeks, but she would not consent to have him notified before the close of the term, and then that she was seriously ill. She was at Newark, N. Y., and when Mr. R. arrived preparations for her funeral were being made. He at once told her and the family that he would take full charge of the case, dismissed the attending physician, to the great astonishment of the family and neighbors, assured her that she was not going to die, that she would live and labor with him.

In two weeks he carried her in his arms to Meridian and left her at her brother's, and she began to improve. He returned to the University, and in a few weeks finished his studies, and was ordained June 12, 1844, in Oswego, N. Y., his father preaching the sermon. The next day his father accompanied him to Meridian, and he and Alzina were married.

In one month they took passage in a fine new brig at Oswego, for a tour of the lakes, for Wisconsin, arriving at Racine in just four weeks. Soon after he accepted the unanimous call of the Baptist church at Whitewater, and were comfortably settled there, remaining there three years, during which time the church prospered and a house of worship was erected. From there they went to Madison, but the winters being too severe for Mrs. Read, they decided to go to California, and in April, 1849, started overland for San Francisco. His library, bedding, clothing and six months provisions were sent around Cape Horn. At Galena, Illinois, they took steamer for St. Louis, Mo. At that time, everywhere, on the rivers, in the cities, the cholera prevailed fatally. At Fort Leavenworth they were detained ten days, and were the guests of Gen. E. V. Sumner. Two days out from Leavenworth Mrs. R. had the cholera! They were providentially detained ten days, and during the time stayed with Rev. Barker and family. He was the Baptist missionary to the Pottawatomie Indians. Mrs. R. recovered so that she was able safely to travel, when the command moved forward.

They had many interesting experiences and incidents on the journey of six weeks to Santa Fé, New Mexico. One was, the head chief of the great Comanche Indians fell most violently in love with pretty Mrs. R., and deliberately proposed to Mr. R. to "swap," and offered to give a papoose with his squaw, and was grievously disappointed because he would not "*swap.*"

Another chief, "Little Bear," of the Kiowas, offered to give them his daughter twelve years of age, whom he wanted to have educated as Mrs. R. was. Neither did they accept this offer.

Arriving at Santa Fé about the middle of July, Mr. R. was importuned by the military governor and his staff and all the principal Americans to locate there, and accept the chaplaincy of the U. S. Army. There was not and never had been a minister of the gospel in the territory. Finding that there was no wagon road beyond Santa Fé—all who were going through were to go on pack mules—the distance being about 1,600 miles, through a hostile Indian country—they thought they must return East and go by water, as their goods had gone that way. But God had a work for them to do in New Mexico, and at once completely shut them in there. Mrs. R. was taken sick and was apparently on the verge of the grave six weeks, so that they were compelled to stay there. Mr. R. accepted the chaplaincy, and at once went to work and a nice chapel was fitted up. Thus commenced the first missionary efforts in that territory. He being the only chaplain of the U. S. Army in the Ninth Military Department, which had twenty-one posts, it was his duty to visit all the garrisons and preach to the troops. Of course this required time, and when away from home Mrs. R. attended to all the work of the mission at headquarters, and also conducted the school numbering seventy pupils, which they established, it being the first academy in New Mexico. When practicable the longest trips were made during vacation, and took him to all parts of New Mexico. In that way he became acquainted with the country, the people and their conditions, temporal and spiritual—their destitution of almost all means and appliances for mental and spiritual improvement.

In 1851, at the earnest solicitation of the A. B. Home Mission society, Mr. and Mrs. Read returned to the East to obtain money and missionaries, preaching and lecturing in all the principal cities, and returned in the spring of 1852 and located missionaries in different places, built a church at Santa Fé, the first Protestant church there. In 1853 formed a church at Albuquerque. He established forty preaching stations on either side of the Rio Grande, which he visited regularly, preaching especially to the Spanish speaking people of the territory; and Mrs. R. conducted the academy and mission in his absence. On one occasion she went in a close carriage alone to Lazuna, about fifty miles, and in crossing a pond in the darkness the carriage body floated from the running gear and turned completely over! Mr. Logan (the Bible-reading colporteur), came to help her out when her head was up against the bottom of the carriage, now bottom side up, and the water up to her chin! Of course she had to get down into the water all over to get out at the door! All this she did heroically and never lost her self-possession for a moment. Another time she was going with Mr. R., in their buggy, drawn by a large, superior mule. They started at sunrise, forded safely the Rio Grande, though not without perils, and, on reaching the Rio Pinco, at 2:30 P. M., they found the water seven feet deep in the channel, and therefore could not cross. They must stay *there*, although it was on the war path of hostile Indians!

Thus reads an extract from a letter from Mr. Read:

"I unharnessed and fastened my mule, shot a rabbit and roasted one hind quarter and for want of something better seasoned it with ashes and ate it with some grapes we brought with us and thus made our dinner and supper together. Our fire was made of a very few little weeds—there being no wood in the vicinity, so that we could not have a fire during the night to scare off the many and ravenous wolves which abounded there. Dear wife was greatly fatigued. We had only a thin lap cover which I spread on the ground for her to recline upon while I sat and stood alternately in the buggy and kept watch. God mercifully protected and preserved us. The next morning I roasted and we ate the other hind quarter of our rabbit, seasoning it with ashes.

"I then found that the stream had gone down two feet during the night leaving only five feet in the channel, so we decided to attempt to cross it. I gave my mule water and harnessed up. I let the buggy-top down, wife sat upon the top of the seat back and her feet on the seat itself. I stood up in the front. My poor mule seemed to realize our danger and hesitated to enter the fearfully dangerous stream. I encouraged her to advance and at length she sprang as far as possible into the water and in an instant was out of sight and the buggy under water! But the momentum she obtained enabled her to soon touch the bottom of the opposite side of the channel (which was not more than twenty feet wide), when she rose to the surface and by the most faithful effort possible she pulled us out and up on the opposite bank! We exclaimed 'God be praised!' We again breathed freely.

"This extraordinary exertion greatly fatigued our mule, who had had nothing to eat since we left home, faring even worse than ourselves. Then the trail was full of deep sand and cobble stones so that we were compelled to go very slowly.

"About noon our poor mule fairly gave out! I sought a place among the sand hills and cedar bushes away from the trail, hoping thereby we might possibly escape the eager eyes of any bloodthirsty savages who might be passing. So while I was hastily unharnessing the faithful, tired and hungry beast, wife attempted to get out of the buggy alone and seemingly forgetting her experiences and discomforts of the last thirty-six hours, *fell* and parted all the ligaments on the inside of her right ankle!!! Oh! Heaven, what was to be done out on this desert? We could only bathe it with a little very muddy water that we had brought along to drink and bind it up with our handkerchiefs. Well, this was a calamity indeed. But we must not tarry long in that dangerous place, so, after an hour in which the mule had a plenty of good, nutritious grass, we started on and late in the night reached our mission station at Lazuna.

"After two days we returned home, dear wife suffering greatly. I summoned several of the army physicians and surgeons, but they could render no relief. Crutches were provided, which she used one year, and then she, in company with Rev. Mr. Shaw and family, went to the States, intending to visit the great medical college of Philadelphia. She had a pleasant and quick journey to Wisconsin, where her only sister, Maria, lived. Her intention was to make a visit and then proceed eastward. Her old family physician offered his services and did what he could, but gave no encouragement of a cure. Meantime she became so debilitated that it was deemed impracticable for her to go farther, and after eight months the Dr. and Bro. Dudley wrote to me to come *at once!*

"The letter was six weeks reaching me, but I instantly commenced preparations for leaving, sitting up all night writing her, Bro. Dudley and the Board, for it was extremely doubtful if I lived to cross the plains in midwinter, with the snow covering the whole country and so cold that buffaloes by thousands froze to death!

"I turned over the care of the mission to Bro. Gorman and started for Santa Fé. Engaged my passage in the mail wagon, for they dared not and would not run a coach. Fare was $150.00. Arriving at St. Louis, after suffering almost incredible hardships and being badly frost-bitten, having lain out in the snow, without fire, shelter or sufficient covering, twenty-four fearfully cold and stormy nights, I found a letter from my wife, and when I reached her she was able to sit up and receive her friends. Oh, *what* relief!

"After a few days we started for Boston. Dr. Hewitt, the celebrated bone-setter, treated her ankle three months, when she was enabled to walk away without her crutches. Meantime her eyes were troubling her, and she was treated for them at the State Infirmary, and so greatly injured that for four years she was nearly blind and most of the time was confined in dark-

(12)

ened rooms. Two celebrated oculists and some of the best physicians in New York attended her for a long time without doing her any good. Everything that money, friends, medical skill and the best possible attention could do was constantly done."

They went to E. Virginia to try the effect of that fine climate. They remained there four years, and Mrs. R. so far recovered her sight as to be able, in July, 1860, to engage with Mr. R. in protracted meeting in Central New York for six months.

During the War of the Rebellion they first went to Washington, and were engaged in furnishing hospitals with necessary goods for the Michigan, Wisconsin and Massachusetts soldiers. Mrs. R. was storekeeper for the N. Y. State Soldiers' Relief association and Mr. R. was preaching in camps, supplying scriptures, tracts and papers to the soldiers in camp and hospitals, caring for the sick, etc., etc.

In June, 1862, Mr. R. started, as a general missionary among the soldiers, for Richmond, but stopped at Savage's Station, nine miles from Richmond, at a large hospital under charge of Dr. Swinburn of Albany.

Hundreds of men were famishing for lack of food and drink, and to each man was given first a little whiskey toddy, then a little cold water, and then some nice gruel. This was continued several days, until all in the camp were taken prisoners, and most of those able to walk were marched to Richmond and confined on Belle Island or in the famous Libby prison. Mr. R. was allowed to remain eleven days, when Jeff Davis learning that at the burial of our deceased soldiers he prayed for the Union army, he ordered him to be confined in Libby prison. He was allowed to stay with the worst sick, wounded and dying. It was his custom to preach three short sermons each evening in the three great wards of the prison.

When sick with typhoid fever he was ordered to the court house, under guard, where he was subjected to a searching examination by a poor old, drunken, bloated apostate, Judge Baxter, for three mortal hours! At the conclusion the judge intimated that he should be condemned to death. A few days after a rebel officer was sent by Jeff Davis to notify him that he was condemned to be hung. The charges against him were, that he was a Yankee, a Union man; that he had great influence with President Lincoln and his cabinet; that he was an Abolitionist; had lived in Virginia; was not a commissioned officer, etc., etc.

Mr. R. told the officer to convey his compliments to Jeff Davis and tell him that he had not hemp enough in his bogus Confederacy to hang him.

So soon as it was known in Washington that he was condemned to be hung, Gen. Burnside was sent out and captured Dr. Broadus of Fredericksburg, Va., who was confined in the old Capitol prison in Washington and kept as hostage for him. Word was sent to Richmond, and his life was spared. He continued his ministries to the sufferers in Libby prison until, in the fall of 1862, he was exchanged for Dr. Broadus and went home feeble and too nearly broken down to return to the post of duty as accounting officer in the Treasury Department. A leave of absence was granted, and still he was unable to remain there.

Congress had recently passed the bill giving a territorial government to Arizona. The President appointed the officers, not one of whom had any personal knowledge of the country, its people, languages or customs, and as he was thoroughly acquainted with that region, he was urged to go. He felt that a trip across the plains would restore his health, and therefore accepted a commission as postmaster for the territory.

Hon. S. P. Chase, Secretary, and F. E. Spinner, U. S. Treasurer, requested him to take out, for circulation, $200,000.00 in paper, postal currency and small bills. This amount he drew at St. Louis, and was to convey it to Santa Fé, N. M. After a long and dangerous trip across the plains, he reached Santa Fé in December, almost in a dying condition in consequence of watching so constantly the money, day and night. However, when relieved of this responsibility, he recovered, and in two weeks was preaching in the meeting house he had built ten years before.

Mrs. R. remained in the East, and if he remained in Arizona she was to go by steamer to San Francisco and he would meet her there. He reached Arizona in January, 1864. Prescott was the site selected for the capital, and there he opened the P. O., chapel and Sunday school.

In August, just when he expected a letter from Mrs. R. that she was about starting for San Francisco, he received the sad, crushing news of her death!

She had gone to New York, expecting to sail June 12, but was taken ill, and after an illness of only three days, fell asleep in Jesus. This was on the anniversary of his ordination, twenty years before. Her remains were sent to Meridian, N. Y., where her funeral was attended the next day, which was the anniversary of their wedding. Thus she was buried where she was born and married.

Mr. R. could not at once leave his field and work in Arizona, but left Dec. 1, arriving in New York in January, 1865. Went to Meridian, then to Hannibal, Mo., where he remained a year.

Since then he has married Miss Lizzie S. Sanderson, and has preached in Virginia, New York, California, Nevada, and is now, 1890, located at El Paso, Texas, as Bible missionary.

Descendants of Asa Smith.

---:o:---

III.

Asa Smith, son of Calvin, gr. son of Matthew 5th, b. Mar. 23, 1788, in E. Haddam, Conn., m. 1st, May 15, 1810, Sally Root (dau. of Daniel Root), who was b. Aug. 19, 1790, in Middlefield, Mass., and d. Sept. 3, 1836. He m. 2d, Mar. 10, 1846, Julia Metcalf (dau. of John Metcalf), who was b. Aug. 2, 1809, in Middlefield, Mass., and d. Oct. 17, 1853. He d. May 6, 1869.

CHILDREN:

(1st marriage.)

I.—Asenath, b. Sept. 17, 1811.
II.—Calvin, b. July 17, 1813, d. Aug. 23 or 25, 1814.
III.—Calvin, b. Dec. 9, 1814.
IV.—Harriet, b. April 6, 1817, d. Jan. 6, 1844.
V.—Almira, b. Sept. 4, 1819.
VI.—Caroline, b. Feb. 11, 1822.
VII.—Harmony, b. June 4, 1824.
VIII.—Angeline, b. Dec. 15, 1828, d. May 7, 1829.
IX.—George, b. July 24, 1834.

1. Asenath Smith, dau. of Asa, gr. dau. of Calvin, b. Sept. 17, 1811, in Middlefield, Mass., m. Sept. 17, 1838 (as second wife, a niece of first wife), Parsons Philip Meacham, who was b. Aug 9, 1795, in Middlefield, Mass., and d. Sept. 6, 1887, in Meridian, N. Y.

His widow still resides in Meridian, N. Y.

CHILDREN:

I.—Harriet, b. April 19, 1840, d. Oct. 11, 1841.
II.—George, b. Sept. 12, 1841, d. Sept 18, 1841.
III.—Charles Hulbert, b. Aug. 7, 1843.
IV.—Francis Wayland, b. Sept. 16, 1845; unmarried.
V.—Cynthia Corinne, b. Sept. 15, 1847, d. April 25, 1869.
VI.—Lawrence Leland, b. April 26, 1852.

Charles Hulbert Meacham, son of Asenath, gr. son of Asa, b. Aug. 7, 1843, m. Mar. 31, 1869, Amy Lovisa Dunbar, who was b. Oct. 26, 1842. They reside in Meridian, N. Y.

CHILDREN:

I.—Harry Bowen, b. Mar. 3, 1871, d. Mar. 30, 1876.
II.—Winfield Dunbar, b. Sept. 5, 1873, d. July 14, 1885.
III.—Carey Leland, b. Sept. 30, 1876, d. Sept. 11, 1886.
IV.—Alice Elma, b. Sept. 21, 1885.

Lawrence Leland Meacham, son of Asenath, gr. son of Asa, b. April 26, 1852, m. January 23, 1890, Minnie Allen Smith (dau. of Clarkson, gr. dau. of Oliver), who was b. July 28, 1862. They reside in Meridian, N. Y., his occupation being that of a farmer.

3. Calvin, son of Asa, gr. son of Calvin, b. Dec. 9, 1814, in Middlefield, Mass., m. 1st, April —, 1837, Harriet Maria Crosier, who was b. March, 1818, and d. March, 1842, leaving one child.

He m. 2d, Sept. 19, 1844, Aurelia Loveland, who was b. Aug. 18, 1822, in Hinsdale, Mass. He d. suddenly, Dec. 10, 1882, in Huntington, Mass., where his widow still resides.

CHILDREN:

(1st marriage.)

I.—Jerome, b. Jan. 7, 1839.

(2d marriage.)

II.—Edwin Dudley, b. Sept. 1, 1845.
III.—Dwight Newton, b. June 19, 1847, d. Aug. 8, 1849.
IV.—Lofton James, b. Mar. 6, 1857.
V.—Frank Wendell, b. Sept. 1, 1860.

Jerome Smith, son of Calvin 4th, gr. son of Asa, b. Jan. 7, 1839, m. June 23, 1868, Jennie Knox, who was b. Dec. 18, 1847, and they now reside in Mason City, Ia.

CHILDREN:

I.—Jessie Maud, b. Nov. 21, 1869.
II.—Lulu Bertha, b. June 13, 1875.
III.—Clarence Hervey, b. April 18, 1878.
IV.—Frank Elmer, b. June 12, 1883, and d. Nov. 18, 1884.

Edwin Dudley Smith, son of Calvin 4th, gr. son of Asa, b. Sept. 1, 1845, m., July 2, 1872, Mary Ella Jones, who was b. Feb. 25, 1851, and d. of consumption Feb. 22, 1888, at her home in Huntington, Mass. He still resides in Huntington.

CHILDREN:

I.—Harry Edwin, b. Aug. 15, 1873.

Lofton James Smith, son of Calvin 4th, gr. son of Asa, b. Mar. 6, 1857, m. Jan. 17, 1877, Alice Mary Newton, who was b. Mar. 8, 1855. They reside in Pittsfield, Mass.

CHILDREN:

I.—Hattie Elsie, b. Oct 24, 1877.

Frank Wendell Smith, son of Calvin 4th, gr. son of Asa, b. Sept. 1, 1860, m. June 7, 1879, Emma Pettit, who was b. Dec. 13, 1860. They reside in Pittsfield, Mass.

CHILDREN:

I.—Maud Harmony, b. Mar. 21, 1880.
II.—Byron Calvin, b. Aug. 27, 1882.
III.—Herbert Wendell, b. June 6, 1885, d. Aug. 23, 1885.
IV.—Arthur C., b. Aug. 2, 1886, d. July 28, 1887.
V.—Walter C., b. Jan. 12, 1888, d. Aug. 24, 1888.
VI.—Emma Louise, b. Feb. 20, 1890.

5. Almira Smith, dau. of Asa, gr. dau. of Calvin, b. Sept. 4, 1819, in Middlefield, Mass., m. Feb. 28, 1850, Benjamin Pratt, who was b. Feb. 28, 1822, in Bloomfield, Maine. She d. Mar. 4, 1889. He resides with his daughter Elma.

They had five children.

CHILDREN:

I.—Clara, b. Aug. 31, 1851, in Northampton, Mass.; unmarried and a retoucher in photography in Los Angeles, California.
II.—Arthur Dwight, b. June 28, 1854.
III.—Sumner Greenleaf, b. Aug. 9, 1855, in Meridian, N. Y., and d. May 26, 1862, in Ripon, Wis.

IV.—Elma Meacham, b. Nov. 12, 1859.

V.—Edwin Dudley, b. Jan. 1, 1863, in Ripon, Wis.; a painter by trade, unmarried, and resides in Los Angeles, California.

Arthur Dwight Pratt, son of Almira, gr. son of Asa, b. June 28, 1854, in Northampton, Mass., m. Oct. 19, 1876, Elizabeth Wakefield, who was b. Jan. 26, 1852, in Summerfield, Ill. He resides in Granite, Colorado, where he is station agent and telegraph operator. They had one child who lived a few hours, Jan. 4, 1881.

Elma Meacham Pratt, dau. of Almira, gr. dau. of Asa, b. Nov. 12, 1859, in Ripon, Wisconsin, m. Aug. 1, 1882, Charles Welborn Jones, a machinist by trade, but now a R. R. engineer living in E. Los Angeles, California. He was b. April 6, 1857, in Augusta, Ga. The following relating to him is of interest:

" Long Island Railroad Co.
Thos. R. Sharp, Receiver.

Gen'l Order }   RECEIVER'S OFFICE,
No. 58.   }   LONG ISLAND CITY, Sept. 15, 1879.

The attention of the service is especially called to the gallant and heroic action of Fireman Chas. Jones, of engine No. 25, train 5, July 23.

In approaching Jamesport the engineer saw a child on the track, blew for brakes and reversed his engine. Fireman Jones, who was on the front of the engine oiling the cylinders, seeing that it would be impossible to stop the train before reaching the child, immediately took a position on the cow-fender and succeeded in grasping it just in time to lift it harmless from the track, thereby saving its life. The child was a little girl about three years of age, the daughter of Mr. Samuel Bartlett, living near Jamesport.

Too much praise cannot be awarded Mr. Jones for his action, and appreciating the ability, courage and good judgment displayed on this and other occasions, his name has been placed by the Master of Machinery on the list for promotion at the first favorable opportunity.

THOS. R. SHARP,
Receiver."

They have two children.

CHILDREN:

I.—Carroll Welborn, b. April 21, 1886.
II.—Edna Almira, b. Sept. 13, 1888.

6. Caroline Smith, dau. of Asa, gr. dau. of Calvin, b. Feb. 11, 1822, m. June 2d or 5th, 1845, Edwin E. Dudley, (son of Sardis Dudley) who was b. Aug. 14, 1822, and d. Nov. 9, 1871.
They had five children.

CHILDREN:

I.—Emma Madora, b. April 7, 1848.
II.—Oakley Smith, b. Feb. 11, 1850.
III.—Helen Estelle, b. July 11, 1852, unmarried, and is supervisor of the Woman's Insane Department of the Philadelphia Hospital, graduating from said hospital Nov., 1889. Previously to her entering the hospital as pupil and nurse, she taught school and music. Having graduated from the Kindergarten Normal School at Washington, D. C., she opened a similar school at Rochester, N. Y., in 1880.
IV.—Lofton Leland, b. July 12, 1854.
V.—Carroll Ide Ernest, b. May 23, 1858.

Emma Madora Dudley, dau. of Caroline, gr. dau. of Asa, b. April 7, 1848, m. May 24, 1875, Francis Marion Pasco, who was b. Sept. 7, 1845.

CHILDREN:

I.—Maurice Dudley, b. Aug. 9, 1885.

Oakley Smith Dudley, son of Caroline, gr. son of Asa, b. Feb. 11, 1850, m. May 5, 1886, Mary Adelaide Dick (of Buffalo, N. Y.), who was b. January 24, 1852. He is a farmer and resides at Meridian, N. Y.

CHILDREN:

I.—Oakley Dick, b. Mar. 2, 1887.

Lofton Leland Dudley, son of Caroline, gr. son of Asa, b. July 12, 1854, m. May 14, 1879, Cora Emma Foote, who was b. June 24, 1858. At the age of seventeen, having a taste for art, he entered the Academy of Design in New York, and in 1877 opened a studio at Worcester, Mass., and painted portraits, and then in the spring of 1878 entered a studio at San Francisco, but his health failed and he returned to the East, and now owns a farm near Auburn, N. Y., and has had a studio in the city for the past five years.

CHILDREN:

I.—Una Foote, b. Oct. 31, 1881.
II.—Edwin Everett, b. Dec. 19, 1882.

Carroll Ide Ernest Dudley, son of Caroline, gr. son of Asa, b. May 23, 1858, m. Feb. 11, 1885, Elizabeth Stevens, who was b. April 17, 1863. He is a farmer, spent some time in Madison, Cal., but now resides in Meridian, N. Y.

CHILDREN:

I.—Jeanie Esther, b. Dec. 12, 1885.
II.—Helen Caroline, b. Oct. 27, 1889.

7. Harmony Smith, dau. of Asa, gr. dau. of Calvin, b. June 4, 1824, in Middlefield, Mass., m. June 28, 1863, Sardis Dudley, who was b. Jan. 10, 1792, and d. Jan. 26, 1876. They had no children, but adopted her brother George's son, Arthur (at the time of his mother's death), three years of age. Name, Arthur Leland Dudley.

Arthur Leland Dudley was b. Sept. 1, 1863, in Middlefield, Mass., and between the ages of three and sixteen attended school in Meridian, N. Y., then entered the high school at Rochester, N. Y., where he graduated in June, 1883, and the following September entered the Rochester University, graduating in June, 1887. The following fall he went to Philadelphia, entered the medical department of the University of Pennsylvania, and graduated in the spring of 1890.

Mrs. Harmony Dudley, up to the time of his graduating this spring, has always made a home for her adopted son, her last address being Philadelphia.

9. George Smith, son of Asa, gr. son of Calvin, b. July 24, 1834, m. 1st, Nov. 12, 1862, Anna Belle Walker, who was b. in 1844, and d. Sept. 1, 1866. He m. 2d, Oct. 23, 1867, Julia

Bartlett, who was b. Dec. 25, 1847. He is a farmer and now resides in Middlefield, Mass. He has one child by first marriage and five by second marriage.

CHILDREN :

(1st marriage.)

I.—Arthur Leland, b. Sept. 1, 1863, and adopted by Sardis and Harmony Dudley when three years of age.

(2d marriage.)

II.—Herbert Clifford, b. April 9, 1870, d. Oct. 1, 1870.
III.—George Ernest, b. April 14, 1872, d. Aug. 19, 1872.
IV.—Edith Maud, b. Dec. 9, 1873.
V.—Walter Asa, b. Dec 1, 1875.
VI.—Kirby W., b. July 11, 1880.

(13)

Descendants of Anna Smith.

---:o:---

IV.

Anna Smith, dau. of Calvin, gr. dau of Matthew 5th, b. April 10, 1790, in Middlefield, Mass., m. Sept. 8, 1808, Daniel Ingham, who was b. June 12, 1787, and d. Dec. 24, 1859, at Portland, Michigan. She d. June 23, 1869.

CHILDREN:

I.—Betsey Anna, b. June 23, 1810.
II.—Temperance Smith, b. Nov. 8, 1812.
III.—Infant, b. April 22, 1814, d. May 9, 1814.
IV.—Fanny Maria, b. Aug. 24, 1816.
V.—Infant, b. March, 1818, d. two weeks old.
VI.—Infant, b. July 24, 1820, d. the same day.
(The above born in Middlefield, Mass.)
VII.—Lawrence Daniel, b. Oct. 1, 1823, at Ira, N. Y., d. Aug. 2, 1827.
VIII.—Ossian, b. in 1827, at Cato, and d. in a few months.
IX.—Oscar Solomon, b. May 15, 1830, at Cato, N. Y.
X.—Mary Latetia, b. Feb. 28, 1833, at Cato, N. Y.

1. Betsey Anna Ingham, dau. of Anna, gr. dau. of Calvin, b. June 23, 1810, in Middlefield, Mass., m. Oct. 23, 1827, at Cato, N. Y., Edward Sandborn, who was b. June 17, 1806. They settled on a new farm in 1843, in Portland, Michigan, then a wilderness, where they lived to clear it up and have a very comfortable home. In 1852, accompanied by his oldest son and

another man, he went to California, by the overland route, then taking three months for the journey. He remained but one year, returning via Panama and New York. He enlisted in the 27th Mich. Infantry, Feb. 15, 1864, and was discharged Jan. 20, 1865, near Petersburg. He d. at Portland, Mich., April 28, 1879. His widow lives with her daughter Latetia in Portland, Michigan.

CHILDREN:

I.—Lawrence, b. May 22, 1829, in Allen, N. Y.
II.—Justus, b. April 16, 1831, " "
III.—Temperance M., b. April 11, 1833, " "
IV.—Columbus, b. June 29, 1837, " "
V.—Josephine Latetia, b. Mar. 20, 1847, in Sebewa, Michigan, and is unmarried, a dressmaker and caring for her mother in Portland, Michigan.
VI.—Morrison, b. July 22, 1849, in Danby, Mich.
VII.—Irvin, b. May 30, 1851, " "

Lawrence Sandborn, son of Betsey A., gr. son of Anna, b. May 22, 1829, in Allen, N. Y., m. 1st, July 9, 1871, at Railroad Flats, California, Libbie Poe, who was b. Feb. 14, 1852, and d. May 29, 1872, at Portland, Mich., leaving one child. He m. 2d, April 2, 1879, Eliza Carr, who was b. Dec. 4, 1850. He spent nearly twenty years in California, prospecting and mining. He is now a farmer and resides on the old homestead in Portland, Mich.

CHILDREN:

(1st marriage.)
I.—Libbie, b. May 20, 1872.

(2d marriage.)
II.—Edna Alvina, b. Feb. 4, 1880.
III.—Alta Almeda, b. June 24, 1882.

IV.—Clifton Allen, b. Aug. 4, 1885.
V.—Ernest Edwin, b. Oct. 13, 1887.

Justus Sandborn, son of Betsey Anna, gr. son of Anna, b. April 16, 1831, in Allen, N. Y., m. May 15, 1854, Harriet Evans, who was b. Aug. 4, 1837. He was a tinsmith. Enlisted in August, 1862, in the 5th Michigan Cavalry; afterwards transferred to the 6th Michigan Cavalry. Discharged July, 1865, and d. Oct. 28, 1865. His widow resides in the northern part of Michigan.

CHILDREN:

I.—Clifford Lawrence, b. Mar. 31, 1855, in Portland, Mich., and d. Dec. 4, 1878, in Salina, Kansas.
II.—Helen Ann, b. Aug. 18, 1856, d. Aug. 9, 1859, in Portland, Mich.
III.—Elzora Sophia, b. Jan. 18, 1858.
IV.—Alice Latetia, b. Sept. 11, 1860.
V.—Bessie Ann, b. Sept. 9, 1865, d. April 26, 1879.

Elzora Sophia Sandborn, dau. of Justus, gr. dan. of Betsey A., b. Jan. 18, 1858, in Portland, Mich., m. April 12, 1882, Andrew Traviss, a farmer, who was b. May 9, 1850, and in 1890 resided at Sherman, Mich.

CHILDREN:

I.—Bessie Elzora, b. Oct. 31, 1884.
II.—Clifton Andrew, b. Oct. 4, 1888.

Alice Latetia Sandborn, dau. of Justus, gr. dan. of Betsey A., b. Sept. 11, 1860, in Rockford, Mich., m. Nov. 26, 1880, Clinton

Joshua Smith, a blacksmith, who was b. April 19, 1858, in Andover, Ohio, and in 1890 resided at Sherman, Mich.

CHILDREN:

I.—Clifford Ingham, b. Nov. 24, 1881.
II.—Clifton Emery, b. Jan. 5, 1883, d. Jan. 31, 1883.
III.—Estella, b. July 12, 1884.
IV.—Hattie May, b. July 11, 1887.
V.—Mabel Elzora, b. April 30, 1889, d. May 2, 1889.

Temperance Matilda Sandborn, dau. of Betsey A., gr. dau. of Anna, b. April 11, 1833, in Allen, N. Y., m. January 31, 1858, Willard Weld, a farmer, who was b. Jan. 31, 1837, and at present resides in Portland, Mich.

CHILDREN:

I.—Elmer Draper, b. Sept. 26, 1862.
II.—Evren Alta, b. Sept. 15, 1865.

Elmer Draper Weld, son of Temperance M., gr. son of Betsey A., b. Sept. 26, 1862, in Danby, Mich., m. Nov. 21, 1889, Alice Munger, who was b. Sept. 16, 1863. He is a farmer, residing in Portland, Mich.

Columbus Sandborn, son of Betsey A., gr. son of Anna, b. June 29, 1837, in Allen, N. Y., m. Aug. 12, 1860, Sarah Gibbs, who was b. Jan. 4, 1844. He enlisted in 21st Mich. Infantry, Aug. 11, 1862, and the following December was taken prisoner at Stone River and confined in Libby prison one month, when he was exchanged at City Point, and returned to his regiment, and remained until the close of the war. He was in Sherman's march to the sea. In 1890, a farmer residing in Portland, Mich.

CHILDREN:

I.—Chester Edward, b. May 20, 1861, in Danby, Mich.
II.—Helen M., b. Nov. 6, 1862, in Portland, Mich.
III.—Albert Riley, b. April 18, 1866, in Sebewa, Mich.
IV.—Lawrence Watson, b. May 25, 1869, " "
V.—May Birdell, b. May 23, 1871, " "
VI.—Eliza Bell, b. Dec. 23, 1874, d. Sept. 12, 1879.
VII.—Arlie Bell, b. Aug. 28, 1878, in Sebewa, Mich.
VIII.—Alice Bernice, b. Dec. 13, 1884, " "

Chester Edward Sandborn, son of Columbus, gr. son of Betsey A., b. May 20, 1861, in Danby, Mich., m. Feb. 27, 1886, Clara Adelle Traviss (adopted sister of Andrew Traviss), who was b. Oct. 25, 1869. He is a teacher and farmer, and in 1890 resided in Portland, Mich.

CHILDREN:

I.—Jessie, b. Jan. 12, 1888, in Sebewa, Mich.
II.—Harry, b. Dec. 14, 1889, in Odessa, Mich.

Helen M. Sandborn, dau. of Columbus, gr. dau. of Betsey A., b. Nov. 6, 1862, in Portland, Mich., m. Sept. 18, 1883, Rev. James Watson Scoles, an Adventist, who was b. June 23, 1858. They have been located in Washington Ter., in Oakland, Cal., but are at present at Graysville, Tenn. No children.

Albert Riley Sandborn, son of Columbus, gr. son of Betsey A., b. April 18, 1866, in Sebewa, Mich., m. July 28, 1889, Cora Ann Schaupp, who was b. Sept. 24, 1870. He is a teacher and resides in Portland, Mich. No children.

Morrison Sandborn, son of Betsey A., gr. son of Anna, b. July 22, 1849, at Danby, Mich., m. Mar. 22, 1870, Mary Matthews, who was b. Mar. 30, 1851, and d. Aug. 24, 1887, at Baldwin, Mich. He resides in Portland, Mich.

CHILDREN:

I.—Blanche Anna, b. June 16, 1871.
II.—Iva Bernice, b. April 11, 1873, d. Feb. 16, 1875.
III.—Freddie Edward, b. Aug. 13, 1875.
IV.—Eva Rachel, b. Sept. 9, 1877.
* V.—Ernest Barney, b. Jan. 9, 1881.
VI.—George, b. Aug. 23, 1885, d. Sept. 22, 1885.
VII.—Claud Ingham, b. Aug. 27, 1886, d. April 21, 1890.

Irvin Sanborn, son of Betsey A., gr. son of Anna, b. May 30, 1851, in Danby, Mich., m. July 8, 1874, Mrs. Effie Otto (*née* Perry), who was b. ——————. In 1890, resided in Bogue Chitto, Miss., being an engineer in a mill. No children.

2. Temperance Smith Ingham, dau. of Anna, gr. dau. of Calvin, b. Nov. 8, 1812, in Middlefield, Mass., m. March 18, 1840, Justus S. Sandborn (bro. of Edward), a farmer and mechanic, who was b. Dec. 4, 1808, and d. Aug. 31, 1888. Before her marriage, she was a successful teacher for twelve years, and now resides in Portland, Mich.

CHILDREN:

I.—Josephine A., b. June 9, 1843, in Allen, N. Y.
II.—Rosalie M., b. May 22, 1849, in Portland, Mich.

Josephine Anna Sandborn, dau. of Temperance S., gr. dau. of Anna, b. June 9, 1843, in Allen, N. Y., m. 1st, Jan. 29, 1861, Jasper Davis (brother of Harriet J. Davis), a farmer, who was b. Aug. 22, 1836. He enlisted in 1st Sharpshooters, 27th Mich. infantry, Feb. 1864, and died of disease in a hospital at Washington June 10, 1864, and was buried on Arlington Heights. She m. 2d, July 14, 1867, Jephtha Baldwin Morehouse, a manufacturer, who was b. June 8, 1825. In 1890, resided in Portland, Mich.

CHILDREN:

(1st marriage.)

I.—Evren Anna, b. Jan. 25, 1864, d. Aug. 10, 1864.

(2d marriage.)

II.—Mabel Rosalie, b. Aug. 7, 1872.

Rosalie Marie Sanborn, dau. of Temperance S., gr. dau. of Anna, b. May 22, 1849, at Portland, Mich., m. Oct. 20, 1867, Orlando W. Pettit, a real estate dealer, who was b. Oct. 6, 1846. She is an artist. In 1890 they resided at Grand Rapids, Mich.

CHILDREN:

I.—Lavern Harvey, b. Sept. 10, 1868, d. Oct. 2, 1868.
II.—Vernon Justus, b. May 22, 1880, d. Aug. 24, 1880.

4. Fanny Maria Ingham, dau. of Anna, gr. dau. of Calvin, b. Aug. 24, 1816, in Middlefield, Mass., m. Sept. 22, 1835, Enoch Sandborn (a brother of Edward and Justus S., the three brothers marrying three sisters), a farmer, who was b. July 30,

1816. In 1854 they went to Portland, Mich., where she died May 12, 1862. In August, 1862, he enlisted in the 5th Mich. Cavalry and was discharged May, 1865, and d. Oct. 15, 1874.

CHILDREN:

I.—Mehettable A., b. Sept. 18, 1837, in Allen, N. Y.
II.—Norman T., b. Jan. 28, 1841, in Allen, N. Y.
III.—Anna M., b. Oct 9, 1842, in Allen, N. Y.

Mehettable A. Sandborn, dau. of Fanny M., gr. dau. of Anna, b. Sept. 18, 1837, in Allen, N. Y., m. Aug. 14, 1853, Lyman Ayrault, a merchant, who was b. April 25, 1830, in Allen, N. Y., and in 1854 removed to Dalton, N. Y., where they still reside.

CHILDREN:

I.—Isabelle Bethia, b. July 28, 1855.
II.—Fanny Alzina, b. Oct. 19, 1857.
III.—May Estella, b. April 8, 1860.
IV.—Franklin Lyman, b. Dec. 25, 1862, d. Mar. 13, 1863.
V.—Charles L., b. Aug. 15, 1865, d. Oct. 24, 1885.
He was educated at State Normal School, Geneseo, N. Y.

Isabelle Bethia Ayrault, dau. of Mehettable A., gr. dau. of Fanny M., b. July 28, 1855, in Dalton, N. Y., m. Aug. 25, 1887, Henry Philo Woodworth, a lumber dealer, who was b. July 12, 1847, in Perry, N. Y. She was educated at Buffalo Female Academy, Buffalo, N. Y., and graduated at Ingham University at Leroy, N. Y. She d. Sept. 16, 1888.

CHILDREN:

I.—Lucy Isabelle, b. Sept. 15, 1888, in Marietta, Ohio.

Fanny Alzina Ayrault, dau. of Mehettable A., gr. dau. of Fanny M., b. Oct. 19, 1857, in Dalton, N. Y., educated at Buffalo Female Academy and graduated at Ingham University, Leroy, N. Y., and from College of Fine Arts in June, 1881. She is an artist and now resides in Dalton, N. Y.

May Estella Ayrault, dau. of Mehettable A., gr. dau. of Fanny M., b. April 8, 1860, in Dalton, N. Y., educated at Ingham University and Granger Place School, Canandaigua, N. Y., m. Feb. 23, 1887, Wm. Henry Schoenan, a merchant, who was b. July 12, 1857, in Waterloo, Ontario. No children.

Norman Thomas Sandborn, son of Fanny M., gr. son of Anna, b. Jan. 28, 1841, in Allen, N. Y., m. 1st, March 1, 1859, Mary Elizabeth Dinsmore (cousin of J. B. Dinsmore), who was b. Mar. 1, 1842, and d. Nov. 12, 1862. He m. 2d, Aug. 16, 1863, Harriet Janet Davis (sister of Jasper Davis), who was b. Mar. 22, 1841. He enlisted in 1st Sharpshooters, 27th Mich. infantry, Jan. 20, 1864, and was discharged July 26, 1865. He is now deputy sheriff and resides in Portland, Mich.

CHILDREN:

(2d marriage.)

I.—Lyman Norman, b. Sept. 16, 1866, in Portland, Mich.
II.—Fanny Louisa, b. Jan. 25, 1869, in Portland, Mich.

Fanny Louisa Sandborn, dau. of Norman T., gr. dau. of Fanny M., b. Jan. 25, 1869, in Portland, Mich, m. Feb. 14, 1889, Lewis Collins Gardner, who was b. Dec. 19, 1865. They reside in Portland, Mich.

CHILDREN:

I.—Florence, b. Jan. 27, 1890, in Portland, Mich.

Anna Maria Sandborn, dau. of Fanny M., gr. dau. of Anna, b. Oct. 9, 1842, in Allen, N. Y., m. Dec. 18, 1860, John Berry Dinsmore, then a farmer, now a dealer in boots and shoes, who was b. Jan. 27, 1840. No children. They reside in Portland, Mich.

9. Oscar Solomon Ingham, son of Anna, gr. son of Calvin, b. May 15, 1830, in Cato, N. Y., m. Feb. 20, 1853, Jean Isabella Moore, who was b. May 22, 1838. He began at the age of seventeen to teach in Western New York, graduated at the University of Michigan in 1858, and was engaged in school work in that State until 1871, being principal of high schools, academies, and was city superintendent of schools in Charlotte, Mich. He paid considerable attention to languages, being familiar with thirteen besides the English. From 1871 to 1876 was principal of a high school in Nebraska. Since then has been in California engaged in school work, being superintendent of schools in Alameda four years and president of the Board of Education six years, as well as editor of a newspaper. Besides holding the degree of A. M. from the University of Michigan, he holds the highest credentials issued by the educational department of every State in which he has taught. He is somewhat prominent in musical circles, has contributed many poems to the press, some of which have been set to music and published in music books and in sheet form. A German author, who was collecting the best poems by Pacific Coast authors, to translate and embody in a volume for the use of his own countrymen, honored him by the selection of two poems. His contributions

to the press and his public addresses have been largely educational translations, scientific and less often political, and he has also written many stories for children.

He was possessor of a cane (until stolen from him) which, in the Ingham family, had been transmitted from generation to generation for 250 years, and of which he said: "It (the cane) was highly valued by my father, who was always careful to impress on my mind the importance of keeping it safely in the family, to be transmitted from oldest son to oldest. I much regret its loss." He is now residing in San Diego, Cal.

CHILDREN:

I.—Albrice Oscar, b. Jan. 26, 1855, in Portland, Mich., is a printer, an exceptionally good book and job printer, one of the best in California; has traveled, visiting most of the interesting portions of the Old World, the Sandwich Islands, and nearly all the United States of America. Is now in Tulare, California.

II.—Charles Dane, b. Feb. 2, 1857, d. Sept. 13, 1857.

III.—Herbert Walter, b. April 3, 1858, d. Mar. 10, 1859.

IV.—Arthur Harold, b. Jan. 16, 1860.

V.—Anna Jean, b. Oct. 12, 1863.

VI.—Daniel Alexander, d. in infancy.

VII.—Athol Wm., b. Sept. 8, 1868.

VIII.—Alice Belle, b. Sept. 1, 1871.

Arthur Harold Ingham, son of Oscar S., gr. son of Anna, b. Jan. 16, 1860, at Charlotte, Mich., m. Sept. 26, 1887, Julia Kennedy, who was b. ⸺⸺.

CHILDREN:

I.—Jean May, b. ⸺, d. in 1889.

II.—Vivian I., b. Feb. —, 1890.

Anna Jean Ingham, dau. of Oscar S., gr. dau. of Anna, b. Oct. 12, 1863, in Charlotte, Mich., m. 1st, ——— ——, 1884, Walter Chaplin, who was b. ——— ——, ———, and 2d, ——————————, who was b. ——— ——, ———.

At the age of fifteen she contributed poems to the press, has acted in the capacity of proof reader, telegraph editor and reporter for some of the best dailies in California; is destined to achieve distinction as a writer; has good musical as well as literary ability. Her present residence is Seattle, Wash. Ter.

10. Mary Latetia, or Latetia M., Ingham, dau. of Anna, gr. dau. of Calvin, b. Feb. 28, 1833, in Cato, N. Y., m. Dec. 25, 1848, Carlton Geo. Ayers, a farmer, who was b. June 20, 1820, and now reside in Edmore, Mich.

CHILDREN:

I.—Sarah Latetia, b. Nov. 13, 1851, in Belfast, N. Y., and d. Feb. 17, 1852.
II.—Adelaide, b. Jan. 12, 1853, in Belfast, N. Y.
III.—Sarah Anna, b. April 30, 1856, " "
IV.—Archibald Carlton, b. Feb. 7, 1859, " "
V.—Hattie, b. Oct. 23, 1862, " "
VI.—Latetia Josephine, b. Nov. 7, 1864, " "
VII.—Glen, b. Mar. 23, 1873, in Sebewa, Mich., and d. April 5, 1873, in Sebewa, Mich.

Adelaide Ayers, dau. of Latetia M., gr. dau. of Anna, b. Jan. 12, 1853, in Belfast, N. Y., m. Mar. 24, 1869, Emery Abijah Joslin, a mechanic, who was b. Oct. 26, 1845. He enlisted in 10th Michigan Cavalry, and was discharged Nov. 22, 1865. They now reside in Edmore, Mich.

CHILDREN:

   I.—Cora, b. Mar. 5, 1870, d. June 19, 1881.
  II.—Audrey, b. April 19, 1872.
 III.—Clarence, b. Mar. 23, 1874.
 IV.—Harry, b. Aug. 28, 1880, d. Sept. 16, 1881.
  V.—Hattie May, b. June 22, 1883, d. Aug. 4, 1883.
 VI.—Carl, b. April 28, 1889.

Sarah Anna Ayers, dau. of Latetia M., gr. dau. of Anna, b. April 30, 1856, in Belfast, N. Y., m. Nov. 16, 1871, Justus Mousehunt, a farmer, who was b. Aug. 19, 1839, and d. Feb. 14, 1888. She attended the Adventist College at Battle Creek, Mich., but at present is in Chicago, engaged in missionary and Bible work.

CHILDREN:

  I.—George, b. Sept. 14, 1872, at Orange, Mich., and d. Oct. 15, 1881.
 II.—Glen, b. Oct. 9, 1880, d. Nov. 3, 1880, in Orange, Mich.
III.—Fenton, b. Nov. 11, 1882, at Orange, Mich.

Archibald Carlton Ayers, son of Latetia M., gr. son of Anna, b. Feb. 7, 1859, in Belfast, N. Y., m. July 5, 1878, Myrtie Johnson, who was b. Sept. 16, 1859. He is a barber and resides in Edmore, Mich.

CHILDREN:

  I.—Carl, b. Nov. 9, 1879, in Sebewa, Mich.
 II.—Ethel, b. March 24, 1885, in Ionia, Mich., and d. April 23, 1885.
III.—Ina, b. Mar. 25, 1886, in Ionia, Mich.

Hattie Ayers, dau. of Latetia M., gr. dau. of Anna, b. Oct. 23, 1862, in Belfast, N. Y., m. Aug. 14, 1880, Eugene Sargent, who was b. Oct. 26, 1853. She d. Oct. 17, 1881. No children. He is a farmer at Sebewa, Mich.

Lettie Josephine Ayers, dau. of Latetia M., gr. dau. of Anna, b. Nov. 7, 1864, m. Dec. 5, 1885, Philip Buchanan, a mechanic, who was b. May 8, 1864. They reside at Battle Creek, Mich.

CHILDREN:

I.—Hilah Norine, b. Oct. 17, 1888.
II.—Archie Justus, b. Feb. 14, 1890.

(14)

Descendants of Orrin Smith.

V.

Orrin Smith, son of Calvin, gr. son of Matthew 5th, b. Dec. 31, 1791, in Middlefield, Mass., and d. May 2, 1874, in Cummington, Mass. He m. Sept. 5, 1815, Sally Wheeler Blush, who was b. Oct. 12, 1795, and d. April 25, 1848.

CHILDREN:

I.—Orrin, b. Aug. 31, 1816; name changed to Charles.
II.—Sarah, b. Aug. 31, 1818, d. Oct. 10, 1821.
III.—Corinth, b. May 15, 1820, d. Oct. 10, 1821.
IV.—Maria, b. June 29, 1822, d. May 9, 1849.
V.—Lawrence, b. July 25, 1824.
VI.—Henry, } b. Jan. 12, 1831, d. April 1, 1831.
VII.—Cynthia, } b. Jan. 12, 1831, d. June 22, 1887.

1. Charles Smith, son of Orrin, gr. son of Calvin, b. Aug. 31, 1816, in Middlefield, Mass., m. Mar. 27, 1843, Louisa Combs, who was b. June 27, 1824, in Middlefield, Mass. They reside in "Smith Hollow," Middlefield, Mass.

CHILDREN:

I—Laura Celia, b. Oct. 9, 1844.
II.—Sarah S., b. Dec. 22, 1849.

Laura Celia Smith, dau. of Charles, gr. dau. of Orrin, b. Oct. 9, 1844, in Middlefield, Mass., m. Aug. 23, 1861, F. Melvin Knapp, who was b. Nov. 12, 1838. They reside in Bowen, Colorado.

CHILDREN:

I.—Melvin Smith, b. May 19, 1864.
II.—Jessie Louisa, b. Oct. 27, 1867.
III.—Edmund Ray, b. Jan. 19, 1871.
IV.—Lora Elizabeth, b. Feb. 13, 1881.
V.—Rupert Lent, b. Jan. 17, 1887.

Sarah S. Smith, dau. of Charles, gr. dau. of Orrin, b. Dec. 22, 1849, in Middlefield, Mass., m. Sept. 22, 1869, Lent B. Amos, who was b. Aug. 7, 1847, and d. Nov. 7, 1873. She attended Claverack College, N. Y., where she took the degree of Bachelor of Arts in June, 1879, and was a teacher in that institution seven years. She now resides with her parents. No children.

5. Lawrence Smith, son of Orrin, gr. son of Calvin, b. July 25, 1824, in Middlefield, Mass., m. Nov. 25, 1852, Louisa Wright, who was b. Mar. 23, 1826. He is a farmer and resides in Littleville, Chester, Mass.; P. O. address is Huntington, Mass. For several years he had charge of Wm. Cullen Bryant's place in Cummington, Mass.

CHILDREN:

I.—Elma Meacham, b. June 20, 1856.
II.—Harriet Louise, b. May 8, 1859.

Elma Meacham Smith, dau. of Lawrence, gr. dau. of Orrin, b. June 20, 1856, in Middlefield, Mass.; attended schools in Middlefield and Cummington, Mass.; attended Westfield Normal school one year; graduated at Wesleyan academy, Wilbraham, Mass., in the business course, then went to Eastman's Business college and graduated in penmanship, then taught school in Cummington three terms, and from there went to Siglais Preparatory School in Newburg, N. Y., and taught penmanship one term, then taught penmanship and studied two years at Claverack college and Hudson River institute, Claverack, N. Y., graduating in 1882. She then went to South Hadley Falls, Mass., where she taught penmanship and assisted in the primary school for three years, when she resigned and for four years taught drawing and penmanship in the public schools in Chicopee, Mass., when she resigned to be a student at Pratt institute at Brooklyn, N. Y., in the art department, studying in the Normal art course, preparing to teach form study and drawing. She is now teaching in Springfield, Mass.

Harriet Louise Smith, dau. of Lawrence, gr. dau. of Orrin, b. May 8, 1859, m. May 17, 1888, Fred Porter Stanton, who was b. July 29, 1855. They reside in Huntington, Mass., and he is a dealer in coal, wood, etc.; also is a carman.

CHILDREN:

I.—Helen Louisa, b. Feb. 18, 1890.

7. Cynthia Smith, dau. of Orrin, gr. dau. of Calvin, b. Jan. 12, 1831 (a twin), in Middlefield, Mass., and d. June 22, 1887, of apoplexy, in Rochester, N. Y., where she was practising her profession. The following is from the Rochester Chronicle:

"It is not fitting that a noble character like Dr. Cynthia Smith should pass from earth without mention of her worth. Her profession, to which she brought the ardent love of an enthusiast, with the tender touch and skilful hand of woman, was acquired under difficulties which would have effectually debarred one less earnest from the advantages of a higher education. This singleness of purpose and patient perseverance was carried into her life-work, which had for its aim, not her own aggrandizement nor even pecuniary profit, but the good of mankind. She was the inventor of an admirable surgical appliance which has proved of great value and which might have brought to her fame and fortune had it been properly placed before the public. The writer knows of more than one instance where the lame have been made to walk through her skill. To the poor she not only gave medical advice but freely of her means without hope of other reward than comes to one "who loves his fellow men." She was singularly unworldly and unselfish, with artistic tastes and mental endowments which fitted her to enjoy, in the highest degree, the grand and beautiful in nature. She denied herself all luxury that might lure her from her purpose to do what she could for suffering humanity in her chosen profession. No one could be in her presence without being uplifted from sordid aims and realizing that she indeed lived on a higher plane, for her faith in her Heavenly Father was perfect and unquestioning and a constant inspiration to her friends. The aroma of this pure Christian life will linger long as a sweet memory of her who, "after life's fitful fever," rests in the sleep "He giveth his beloved."

Descendants of Oliver Smith.

---:o:---

VI.

Oliver Smith, son of Calvin, gr. son of Matthew 5th, b. Oct. 28, 1793, in Middlefield, Mass., and d. there Dec. 25, 1881, at that time being the oldest inhabitant. He had been a member of the Baptist church since its organization, June 11, 1818, and was chosen deacon in 1835. He lived about four miles from church, and was invariably at his post of duty. During a series of meetings, a few years before his death, he attended meetings at the church sixty consecutive evenings, walking a good deal of the time. He lived a widower for nearly thirty-three years. He m. Sept. 10, 1816, Fanny Root (dau. of Daniel Root), who was b. June 14, 1795, and d. Jan. 12, 1849.

CHILDREN: (all born in Middlefield.)

    I.—Oliver, b. Oct. 27, 1817, afterwards changed to Milton.
    II.—Fanny, b. Jan. 13, 1820, afterwards changed to Miranda.
    III.—Louisa, b. Feb. 20, 1822.
    IV.—Julia, b. Jan. 30, 1824.
    V.—Franklin, b. April 13, 1826.
    VI.—Wayland, b. July 19, 1831, d. Aug. 25, 1852.
    VII.—Electa, b. Jan. 8, 1834, d. Feb. 3, 1889.
    VIII.—Jane, b. Jan. 29, 1836.
    IX.—Clarkson, b. July 10, 1838.
    X.—Zilpha, b. Jan. 27, 1841, d. Jan. 30, 1872, in Winona, Minn.

1. Milton Smith, son of Oliver, gr. son of Calvin, b. Oct. 27, 1817, in Middlefield, Mass., m. May 2, 1843, Mary Smith Browning, who was b. Sept. 14, 1818, and d. Nov. 11, 1881. He resides in Mittineague, Mass.

CHILDREN:

I.—Justus Browning, b. Dec. 24, 1844.
II.—Clarence Emmons, b. Nov. 21, 1846.
III.—Julia Louisa, b. Dec. 22, 1848, d. Jan. 4, 1871.
IV.—Dwight, b. Feb. 5, 1851, d. Sept. 7, 1872.
V.—Wayland Francis, b. July 26, 1853.
VI.—Alice Amanda, b. Jan. 30, 1857.
VII.—Mary Emmons, } b. Mar. 26, 1859.
VIII.—Fannie Root,

Justus Browning Smith, son of Milton, gr. son of Oliver, b. Dec. 24, 1844, in Middlefield, Mass., m. June 27, 1873, Ella Loveland, who was b. July 10, 1845. They have no children except an adopted son, Leslie. Mr. Smith is one of the firm of Smith Bros., who keep a general store in Mittineague, Mass.

Clarence Emmons Smith, son of Milton, gr. son of Oliver, b. Nov. 21, 1846, in Middlefield, Mass., m. Sept. —, 1883, Addie Eliza Fuller, who was b. April 25, 1856. They reside in Mittineague, and he is one of the firm of Smith Bros., who are engaged in the mercantile business.

CHILDREN:

I.—Carl Browning, b. July 20, 1884.

Wayland Francis Smith, son of Milton, gr. son of Oliver, b. July 26, 1853, in Middlefield, Mass., m. Feb. 18, 1875, Lillie C.

Ingham, who was b. Dec. 17, 1854, in Middlefield, Mass. Their address is Mittineague, Mass.

CHILDREN:

I.—Dwight Ingham, b. Aug. 21, 1878.
II.—Effie Luella, b. Sept. 15, 1880.

Alice Amanda Smith, dau. of Milton, gr. dau. of Oliver, gt. gr. dau. of Calvin, b. Jan. 30, 1857, in Middlefield, Mass., m. May 30, 1882, Edwin Smith (son of Ebenezer, gr. son of Calvin), who was b. Oct. 23, 1856, in Middlefield, Mass. Their address is Mittineague, Mass.

CHILDREN:

I.—Mary Browning, b. July 3, 1889, d. Jan. 6, 1890.
They adopted her sister Mary's child, Winfred Emmons, b. June 3, 1887.

Mary Emmons Smith, dau. of Milton, gr. dau. of Oliver, b. Mar. 26, 1859, m. April 23, 1884, Arthur P. Combs, who was b. Dec. 12, 1859, in Middlefield, Mass. He is engaged in mercantile business in Springfield, Mass. She d. June 21, 1887, leaving two children, the youngest being immediately adopted by her older sister, Alice.

CHILDREN:

I.—Louis Eugene, b. Aug. 24, 1885.
II.—Winfred Emmons, b. June 3, 1887.

Fannie Root Smith, dau. of Milton, gr. dau. of Oliver, b. Mar. 26, 1859, in Middlefield, Mass., m. April 23, 1884, Lyman Ebenezer Smith, (brother of Edwin, before mentioned, son of Ebenezer, gr. son of Calvin), who was b. Aug. 31, 1858, in Middlefield, Mass. Their address is Mittineague, Mass. No children.

2. Miranda Smith, dau. of Oliver, gr. dau. of Calvin, b. Jan. 13, 1820, in Middlefield, Mass., m. Dec. 29, 1842, Albert Olmstead, who was b. April 13, 1814, and d. Nov. 30, 1854. She resides in Wethersfield, Conn.

CHILDREN:

I.—Albert Franklin, b. Nov. 30, 1844.
II.—Julia Isabel, b. Mar. 6, 1847.
III.—Parks, b. Sept. 16, 1852, d. Sept. 10, 1853.
IV.—Fannie Alberta, b. Mar. 4, 1855. She resides in Wethersfield, Conn., and is a music teacher.

Albert Franklin Olmstead, son of Miranda, gr. son of Oliver, b. Nov. 30, 1844, m. Oct. —, 1873, Jennie Elizabeth Olmstead, who was b. Sept. —, ———.

CHILDREN:

I.—Alice Jennie, b. May 24, 1874.
II.—Albert Wm., b. Sept. 26, 1875.
III.—Edith Maria, b. Oct. 30, about 1878.

Julia Isabel Olmstead, dau. of Miranda, gr. dau. of Oliver, b. Mar. 6, 1847, in Hazardville, Conn., m. Oct. 12, 1865, Charles Alexander Bedford, who was b. July 7, 1836, in Esopus, N. Y., and they reside at Esopus.

CHILDREN:

I.—Albert Morgan, b. Jan. 13, 1867, at Hazardville, Conn.
II.—Louisa Horton, b. Sept. 30, 1873, in Esopus, N. Y.
III.—Harry R., b. Dec. 20, 1874,   "   "

3. Louisa Smith, dau. of Oliver, gr. dau. of Calvin, b. Feb. 20, 1822, in Middlefield, Mass., m. Dec. 16, 1858, Elisha Strong, who was b. Oct. 26, 1820, and d. May 17, 1890, in Northampton, Mass. Her address is at present Northampton, Mass. No children.

4. Julia Smith, dau. of Oliver, gr. dau. of Calvin, b. Jan. 30, 1824, in Middlefield, Mass., m. Feb. 28, 1850, Sylvester Bartlett, who was b. June 6, 1821, and d. Feb. 1, 1885. He was a carpenter and builder. She makes it her home at her daughter's in Springfield, Mass.

CHILDREN:

I.—Holliston Irving, b. June 1, 1851, d. Nov. 27, 1852.
II.—Fannie Edith, b. July 28, 1855.

Fannie Edith Bartlett, dau. of Julia, gr. dau. of Oliver, b. July 28, 1855, m. June 6, 1877, Albert Clement Hayes, who was b. Mar. 1, 1850. They reside in Springfield, Mass. He is an insurance broker, and is also employed by Boston and Albany railroad.

CHILDREN:

I.—Edith May, b. Jan. 17, 1879.
II.—Ethel June, b. Feb. 14, 1881.
III.—Irving Clement, b. Oct. 12, 1885.

5. Franklin Smith, son of Oliver, gr. son of Calvin, b. April 13, 1826, in Middlefield, Mass., m. Dec. 3d or 4th, 1854, Ann Spencer, who was b. Nov. 24, 1826, in Middlefield, Mass. In 1847 he went to Enfield, Conn., to learn the trade of a tinsmith, and in 1854 commenced business in company with his brother-in-law, Albert Olmstead, also dealing in stoves and tinware, etc., and continued in that business and paper stock for sixteen years, when he sold out and has since been engaged in insurance business, his present address being Hazardville, Conn., which is in the town of Enfield, Conn.

CHILDREN:

I.—Jessie Mary, b. Nov. 14, 1856.
II.—Charles Nelson, b. June 14, 1859.
III.—Eugene Oliver, b. Oct. 14, 1863.
IV.—Louis C., b. April 1, 1871.

Jessie Mary Smith, dau. of Franklin, gr. dau. of Oliver, b. Nov. 14, 1856, m. 1st, Albert R. Law, Oct. 27, 1881. He was

b. Oct. 14, 1856, and d. Mar. 3, 1882. She m. 2d, May 16, 1888, William A. Smith, who was b. May 4, 1845. They reside in Hazardville, Conn. No children.

Charles Nelson Smith, son of Franklin, gr. son of Oliver, b. June 14, 1859, m. Sept. 1, 1885, Julia J. Hannagan, who was b. Oct. 4, 1862. They reside in Thompsonville, Conn.

CHILDREN:

I.—Anna Gertrude, b. Mar. 15, 1886.

7. Electa Smith, dau. of Oliver, gr. dau. of Calvin, b. Jan. 8, 1834, in Middlefield, Mass., where she spent her younger days. She was a bright and gifted woman, and for twenty-five years taught in the public schools in Middlefield and Becket in Massachusetts, and in Enfield and Manchester in Connecticut and other places, until her health failed. For four years previous to her death, which occurred Feb. 3, 1889, she was a confirmed invalid, and lived with her sister Louisa, in Northampton, Mass., and took no nourishment except milk. For the last two years her sight and hearing had been gone, and she was as helpless as a little child.

8. Jane Smith, dau. of Oliver, gr. dau. of Calvin, b. Jan. 29, 1836, in Middlefield, Mass., m. Nov. 2, 1856, John Smith, who was b. Dec. 26, 1833. She was an invalid for many years previous to her death, which occurred Oct. 28, 1888. He is a carpenter and resides in Los Angeles, Cal., though most of the time he is among the mountains on account of asthma.

CHILDREN:

I.—Oliver Carey, b. Mar. 11, 1858; resides in Los Angeles, Cal., is a carpenter and is also license inspector for the city.
II.—Estella May, b. Jan. 10, 1860.

9. Clarkson Smith, son of Oliver, gr. son of Calvin, b. July 10, 1838, in Middlefield, Mass., m. Oct. 16, 1861, Roxanna Gowdy, who was b. Sept. 28, 1839. They reside in Worcester, Mass. He is janitor for one of the buildings owned by the Worcester Technical Institute.

CHILDREN:

I.—Minnie Allen, b. July 28, 1862.
II.—Clayton Oliver, b. June 30, 1870.
III.—Fannie Electa, b. July 26, 1875.

Minnie Allen Smith, dau. of Clarkson, gr. dau. of Oliver, gt. gr. dau. of Calvin, b. July 28, 1862, m. Jan. 23, 1890, Lawrence Leland Meacham (son of Asenath, gr. son of Asa, gt. gr. son of Calvin), who was b. April 26, 1852. They reside in Meridian, N. Y., and he is a farmer.

10. Zilpha Smith, dau. of Oliver, gr. dau. of Calvin, b. Jan. 27, 1841, in Middlefield, Mass., and d. of typhoid fever in Winona, Minn., Jan. 30, 1872.

Descendants of Ambrose Smith.

VII.

Ambrose Smith, son of Calvin, gr. son of Matthew 5th, b. June 17, 1796, in Middlefield, Mass., and d. Aug. 20, 1859. He m. May 13, 1819, Nancy Alderman, who was b. Jan. 19, 1797, and d. Feb. 24, 1888.

CHILDREN:

I.—Nancy, b. Oct. 31, 1820, d. Mar. 1, 1854.
II.—Mary Cleantha, b. Aug. 21, 1822.
III.—Clarissa Anna, b. Feb. 5, 1824.
IV.—Betsey, b. Dec. 4, 1827.
V.—Ambrose Oakley, b. Aug. 4, 1829.
VI.—Henry, b. Jan. 5, 1832; was collector of customs at Apalachicola, Florida, and d. July 18, 1873.

2. Mary Cleantha Smith, dau. of Ambrose, gr. dau. of Calvin, b. Aug. 21, 1822, m. May 4, 1843, Dr. Wm. K. Otis, who was b. Jan. 3, 1819, in Wilbraham, Mass., and d. July 18, 1880, of malarial fever, in Willimantic, Conn. She resides in Springfield, Mass.

CHILDREN:

I.—Isadore, b. May 10, 1845, d. Jan. 21, 1847.
II.—Wm. Lofton, b. Sept. 10, 1847, d. Nov. 29, 1850.
III.—Ella Mariah, b. Nov. 20, 1849, d. July 7, 1851.

3. Clarissa Ann Smith, dau. of Ambrose, gr. dau. of Calvin, b. Feb. 5, 1824, m. Sept. 16, 1852, Charles Chandler Thompson, who was b. Sept. 14, 1823. They reside in Longmeadow, Mass.

CHILDREN:

I.—Charles Grafton, b. Sept. 29, 1855.
II.—Lora C., b. April 21, 1857, d. Nov. 25, 1872.
III.—Henry Sumner, b. Dec. 17, 1863.

4. Betsey, dau. of Ambrose, gr. dau. of Calvin, b. Dec. 4, 1827, m. Nov. 27, 1847, Alvah B. Pierce, who was b. Feb. 19, 1826, and d. Sept. 19, 1851. She resides in Springfield, Mass.

CHILDREN:

I.—McKendrie B., b. Mar. 17, 1850, and d. Oct. 3, 1871. He was killed by the caving in of a well he was digging.

Descendants of Obadiah Smith.

——:o:——

VIII.

Obadiah Smith, son of Calvin, gr. son of Matthew 5th, b. May 20, 1798, in Middlefield, Mass., and d. Aug. 14, 1853. He was a farmer and lived in Middlefield, Mass. He m. Sept. 9, 1824, Seviah Tower, who was b. Oct. 19, 1798, and d. Jan. 9, 1877.

CHILDREN:

I.—Lorinda, b. July 6, 1825.
II.—Clarinda, b. April 8, 1828.
III.—Matilda, b. June 25, 1831.
IV.—Amanda, b. May 28, 1833.

1. Lorinda Smith, dau. of Obadiah, gr. dau. of Calvin, b. July 6, 1825, m. 1st, Aug. 27, 1847, Rev. Edward King, who was b. Feb. 5, 1824; (date of death unknown.) She m. 2d, Aug. 28, 1860, Samuel Ware Fisher, who was b. Dec. 14, 1817, and d. Jan. 6, 1884, in Springfield, Mass. She was a teacher the most of her life. She died in Springfield, Mass., April 6, 1885.

CHILDREN:

(1st marriage.)

I.—Edward Smith, b. Sept. 8, 1848; has now dropped the "Smith," and is known only as Edward King.

(2d marriage.)

II.—Herbert, b. May 26, 1861, d. July, 1861.
III.—Charlotte Bronté, b. Aug. 21, 1864.
IV.—Mary L., b. Feb. 7, 1866.
V.—Harry, b. Nov. 21, 1868; was a student at Mr. Moody's school, Mt. Hermon.

Edward King, son of Lorinda, gr. son of Obadiah, b. Sept. 8, 1848, in Middlefield, Mass.; was privately educated, but in this manner went through the entire course of study in vogue at Williams College. When only seventeen years of age he entered the office of the Springfield (Mass.) Union as a compositor, becoming almost immediately local editor. Samuel Bowles, then editor of the Springfield Republican, noticed his work, and being impressed with his ability, sent him to Europe as a special correspondent. This was in 1867, and on his return he became literary editor of the Republican. In the following year he edited the Evening News, an offshoot of the Republican. In 1869 he was again in Europe as special correspondent of the Boston Journal, and in that capacity followed the Franco-Prussian war and the incidents of the Paris commune in 1870. Until 1872 he was a member of the Journal editorial staff. He then traveled through the South, in 1873, accompanied by an artist, and contributed to Scribner's Monthly a series of illustrated articles on that section, entitled "The Great South." During this journey he traveled 25,000 miles, of which 1,200 was on horseback. Among the places visited was New Orleans, and by some the discovery of George W. Cable was considered his greatest achievement, for here he became acquainted with Mr. Cable, and was so impressed with his talents that he took it upon himself to forward some of Mr. Cable's manuscripts to Dr. Holland, with the strongest kind of recommendation. In this way the author of "Old Creole Days" got his chance at the public.

In 1875 he went to Europe again, and from Paris corresponded with American papers. In 1876 he represented the

Boston Journal at the Centennial exhibition in Philadelphia, and in 1877, being again in Europe, he wrote letters for the American press from the seat of war in Bulgaria.

Mr. King has made an enviable reputation by his poems, " Echoes from the Orient," and " A Venetian Lover," and "Paul Graine." Among other works in book form, he has published, " My Paris " (1868), " Kentucky's Love," a novel (1872), " The Great South " (1874), French Political Leaders (1876), Europe in Storm and Calm (1885). He is now in New York, connected with "The Morning Journal."

Charlotte Bronté Fisher (half sister of Edward King), dau. of Lorinda, gr. dau. of Obadiah, b. Aug. 21, 1864, m. Dec. 19, 1889 (at Highland Falls, N. Y., at the residence of John Bigelow, the historian and ex-Minister to France), John McGhie, who was b. April 23, 1863, in Liverpool, England. His father and uncle and brother are the sole male survivors, in direct line, of the head of the southron or border house of McGhie of Balmaghie, Kirkculbrightshire, Scotland. He has been closely connected with the " Westminster Review" of London, and is an A. A. of University of Oxford. They reside in Brooklyn, N. Y.

Mary L. Fisher (half sister of Edward King), dau. of Lorinda, gr. dau. of Obadiah, b. Feb. 7, 1866, m. Dec. 19, 1889 (at same place and by the same minister), George Cornelius Eighme, who was b. Aug. 24, 1863, in Cambria, Niagara Co., N. Y. He is a dentist, and now resides in Bridgeport, Conn. He spent his early school days in the Cambria school, then took a college preparatory course at the Lockport Union school, and then began the study of medicine in Lockport, N. Y., which he continued two years, then changed and took up the study of dentistry in the office of Dr. A. J. Allen, Lockport, and afterwards took the full course of the Pennsylvania College of Dental Surgery, in Philadelphia, graduating and taking the degree of D. D. S., Feb. 26, 1887, and the same spring established a dental office in the city, where he is still located.

2. Clarinda Smith, dau. of Obadiah, gr. dau. of Calvin, b. April 8, 1828, m. Feb. 4, 1851, Clark Allen Corey, who was b. May 3, 1826. She d. Nov. 17, 1862. He lives in Suffield, Conn.

CHILDREN:

I.—James Allen, b. Dec. 13, 1851.
II.—Jessie, b. Dec. 8, 1856, d. July 18, 1857.
III.—Effie Sarah, b. Oct. 14, 1858.
IV.—Grace Amanda, b. Oct. 10, 1860. Her address is West Simsbury, Conn.

Effie Sarah Corey, dau. of Clarinda, gr. dau. of Obadiah, b. Oct. 14, 1858, in Becket, Mass., m. Mar. 3, 1881, Frederick Austin Scott, who was b. April 21, 1855. Think their address is Suffield, Conn.

CHILDREN:

I.—Walter Eugene, b. June 10, 1882, d. Sept. 11, 1883.
II.—Herbert Allen, b. Aug. 2, 1883, d. Oct. 16, 1883.
III.—Clarence Burton, b. Sept. 7, 1884.
IV.—Grace Ella, b. Jan. 12, 1887.
V.—Allen Corey, b. Oct. 1, 1889.

3. Matilda Smith, dau. of Obadiah, gr. dau. of Calvin, b. June 25, 1831, m. Mar. 29, 1853, Joel Bigelow Mellen, who was b. Jan. 24, 1821, in Arlington, Vt., and d. Feb. 24, 1866, in Newberne, N. C. He served two or three years in the War of the Rebellion. She d. Sept. 21, 1857.

CHILDREN:

I.—William Albro, b. Nov. 20, 1854. He was adopted when quite young by A. B. Curtis of Worthington, Mass., and his name changed. Some of the time he is there and has also worked in Dalton, Mass.

II.—Jane R., b. Jan. 8, 1857, d. Oct. 13, 1857.

4. Amanda Smith, dau. of Obadiah, gr. dau. of Calvin, b. May 28, 1833, m. July 4, 1878, John Fay, who was b. July 4, 1832. They have no children and reside in Chester, Mass.

Descendants of Sally Smith.

IX.

Sally Smith, dau. of Calvin, gr. dau. of Matthew 5th, b. Feb. 15, 1800, in Middlefield, Mass., m. Sept. 20, 1820, Parsons Philip Meacham, who was b. Aug. 9, 1795, and d. Sept. 6, 1887. She d. Feb. 5, 1836. Their residence was Meridian, N. Y.

CHILDREN:

I.—Parsons P., b. Aug. 27, 1821, d. Aug. 27, 1821.
II.—Franklin Smith, b. Oct. 19, 1823, d. Aug. 11, 1826.
III.—Wm. Irving, b. Nov. 7, 1825, d. Aug. 11, 1829.
IV.—Sarah Elma, b. Oct. 27, 1829; resides in Meridian, N. Y.
V.—Cleantha Mary, b. July 4, 1834; resides in Meridian, N. Y.

Descendants of Ebenezer Smith.

XI.

Ebenezer Smith, son of Calvin, gr. son of Matthew Smith 5th, b. Aug. 10, 1804, in Middlefield, Mass., m. 1st, Nov. 5, 1829, Sibyl Pease, who was b. Jan. 27, 1810, and d. July 20, 1855. He m. 2d, Jan. 1, 1856, Mrs. Sarah A. Hawes (*née* Hazeltine), who was b. Oct. 24, 1819. He d. Mar. 30, 1869. His widow m. Harvey Root of Middlefield. He died and she resides in Mittineague, Mass.

CHILDREN:

(1st marriage.)

I.—Morgan, b. Feb. 16, 1831, d. Dec. 11, 1860. He was educated in the common schools of Middlefield, Mass. (where he was born), and at Williston Seminary, Easthampton, Mass., and for five years was a teacher, then went West, located at Elgin, Ill., engaged in farming, and by overwork in the harvest field brought on a turn of bleeding at the lungs, and died of consumption in Elgin, and by request was buried at Middlefield, Mass. He taught school in Middlefield and Feeding Hills, Mass.

II.—Albert, b. Sept. 30, 1832.
III.—William, b. Nov. 24, 1834, d. Sept. 19, 1853.
IV.—Martha, b. Jan. 2, 1837, d. May 18, 1856.
V.—Howard, b. Nov. 4, 1838.
VI.—Rosina, b. May 30, 1842, d. Aug. 3, 1855.

(2d marriage.)

VII.—Edwin, } b. Oct. 23, 1856.
VIII.—Edson. } b. Oct. 23, 1856, d. April 7, 1864.
IX.—Lyman Ebenezer, b. Aug. 31, 1858.

X.—Henry Wilson, b. May 28, 1867; resides in Mittineague, Mass.

2. Albert Smith, son of Ebenezer, gr. son of Calvin, gt. gr. son of Matthew 5th, b. Sept. 30, 1832, in Middlefield, Mass., m April 7, 1857, Mary Ann Smith (dau. of Matthew 7th, gr. dau. of Matthew 6th, gt. gr. dau. of Matthew 5th), who was b. Aug. 13, 1832, in Middlefield, Mass. He is a farmer, and they reside in Elgin, Ill. Before his marriage he taught school in Peru, Worthington Corners, East Becket and Huntington, Mass., and after his marriage, in Prairie du Chien, Wis., and Elgin, Ill. When through teaching he turned his attention to farming, first renting a farm for four years, which he afterwards bought and on which he now lives.

CHILDREN:

I.—Ella Florence, b. Mar. 20, 1859, d. Jan. 19, 1886.
II.—Albert Matthew, b. April 4, 1863.
III.—Carrie Birdie, b. Mar. 29, 1873, d. June 26, 1873.

Albert Matthew Smith, son of Albert, gr. son of Ebenezer b. April 4, 1863, m. Sept. 30, 1884, Clara Stringer, who was b. June 17, 1861. They reside in Elgin, Ill.

CHILDREN:

I.—Edwin Harold, b. Mar. 31, 1887, d. April 22, 1889.
II.—Albert Leo, b. Aug. 3, 1890.

5. Howard Smith, son of Ebenezer, gr. son of Calvin, b. Nov. 4, 1838, in Middlefield, Mass., m. May 31, 1871, Maggie E. Ford, who was b. Mar. 24, 1848. He is a farmer and they reside on the old homestead in Middlefield, Mass.

CHILDREN:

I.—Rosina Maggie, b. Feb. 6, 1874; a teacher and resides in Middlefield, Mass.
II.—Flora Lena, b. May 13, 1876.
III.—Bernard Howard, b. Dec. 16, 1878.

7. Edwin Smith, son of Ebenezer, gr. son of Calvin, b. Oct. 23, 1856, in Middlefield, Mass., m. May 30, 1882, Alice Amanda Smith (dau. of Milton, gr. dau. of Oliver, gt. gr. dau. of Calvin), who was b. Jan. 30, 1857. They reside in Mittineague, Mass.

CHILDREN:

I.—Mary Browning, b. July 3, 1889, d. Jan. 6, 1890.

(Adopted child.)

II.—Winfred Emmons, b. June 3, 1887; was adopted after the death of her sister Mary. (See descendants of Oliver Smith.)

9. Lyman Ebenezer Smith, son of Ebenezer, gr. son of Calvin, b. Aug. 31, 1858, in Middlefield, Mass., m. April 23, 1884, Fannie Root Smith (sister of Alice, before mentioned), dau. of Milton, gr. dau. of Oliver, gt. gr. dau. of Calvin, who was b. Mar. 26, 1859, in Middlefield, Mass. They have no children, and their address is Mittineague, Mass.

Descendants of Sarah Smith.

——:o:——

Sarah Smith, dau. of Matthew Smith 5th, gr. dau. of Matthew 4th, b. Aug. 14, 1764, (?) m. after 1802, John Parke, as his second wife. They had no children, and no record of dates, except these mentioned, could be ascertained.

INDEX.

A

Aborn, Sarah E.......... 80
Ackley, Asa............. 37
" Benjamin........ 37
" Catharine C.....159
" Edwin C........159
" Elizabeth.......... 37
" Ellen L..........159
" Eveline C.......135
" Frances E.......158
" George..........159
" Howard.....158, 159
" Howard P.......159
" Joseph O........135
" Matilda......... 37
" Oliver.......... 37
" Polly........... 37
" Rebecca......... 37
" Ruthy...........123
" Sally........... 37
" Sophia S........135
" Susan........... 37
" Temperance......
  135, 136, 137
" Wallace H.......159
Adams, John Quincy..... 55
" Martha L........119
" Mary............114
" Thomas.......11, 14
Alderman, Nancy........227
Allen, A. J., M. D.......233
" Nancy...........151
Ames, Lent B...........212
" Sarah S.........212
Anable, Anna...........163
" Asenath......41, 163
Anderson, Eliza......... 29
" George....... 29
Andrew, John A......... 76
Andrews, Jedediah....... 28
Archibald, Arthur.......1 28

Archibald, Bessie........128
" Florence A....127
" Forrester R....128
" Fred.........128
" James........127
" Lee..........128
Arnold, Elizabeth.....12, 24
" Josiah..12, 13, 14, 24
" Josiah, Jr.,....12, 24
" Lydia......12, 13, 24
Atkins, Linus........... 29
" Marintha......... 29
Awai, Mr...........99, 100
Ayers, Adelaide.........206
" Archibald C..206, 207
" Carl.............207
" Carlton G........206
" Ethel............207
" Glen.............206
" Hattie.......206, 208
" Ina..............207
" Latetia J.....206, 208
" Latetia M. 206, 207, 208
" Myrtie J.........207
" Sarah A......206, 207
" Sarah L..........206
Ayrault, Chas. L........202
" Fanny A....202, 203
" Franklin L......202
" Isabelle B.......202
" Lyman..........202
" May E......202, 203
" Mehettable A.202,203
Ayres, William H....... 34

B

Bacon, Rev. Elijah.......167
" Huldah..........167
Bailey, Sarah H......... 20
Baird, Berton G......... 22
" Frederick......... 22

Baird, Frederick N....... 22
" Gustavus J........ 22
" Hannah E........ 22
" Helen P.......... 22
" Lerusa M......... 22
" Mabel M......... 22
" Rosalthe L........ 23
" Roxanna C........ 22
" Sarah L.......... 22
" Solomon T........ 22
" William J......... 22
Baker, Dorothy..........113
Baldwin, Ashbel C......130
" Ashbel W......131
" Forrester B.....131
" Ida K..........131
" Ralph A........131
" Sophia S...130, 131
Barker, Rev............174
Barnaby, Lizzie A........ 83
" Olive L........ 83
" W. G.......... 83
Barnes, Mary........... 27
Bartlett, Fannie E...221, 222
" Holliston I......221
" Julia...191, 221, 222
" Samuel..........187
" Sylvester........221
Barton, Adaline S........156
Baxter, Judge............178
Bayley, C. C............. 62
Beckwith, Francis........ 34
Bedford, Albert M.......221
" Chas. A........221
" Harry R.......221
" Julia I........221
" Louisa H.......221
Beebe, Hannah.......... 28
" Levi............. 21
" Martha C......... 21
Bennett, Abby E........120
" Amy H........120
" David M........172
" George S.......120
" Gladys G........172
" Helen A........172

Bennett, Temperance A...120
" William H......120
Berthold, Anna..........156
Bigelow, John...........233
Blankinton, Martha S.... 21
" Mr......... 21
Bliss, Mary M........... 95
Blush, Sally W..........211
Boise, L. D............. 80
Bonfoey, Freeman....... 83
" Lizzie A........ 83
" Lucy F......... 83
" Nelson R....... 83
" Nora H........ 83
Booge, John............. 7
Bowles, Samuel..........232
Boyd, Elizabeth.........135
" Ellen S..........136
" Eveline C. 135, 136, 137
" Frederic A........136
" Frederic Wm. O...136
" Isabel W.....136, 137
" Sarah J.........136
" Wm. B......135, 136
Brainard, Joseph........141
" Sophia.......141
" Stephen....... 12
Brewer, Mary.......... 48
Broadus, Dr............179
Brockway, Mary........ 24
Browning, Mary S......218
Brush, Alice S.......... 21
" Georgie..........158
" Hazel B.........158
" Lottie M........158
" Louis............158
" Mr.............. 21
Bryant, Wm. Cullen.....212
Buchanan, Archie J......208
" Hilah N......208
" Latetia J......208
" Philip.......208
Buckley, John........... 11
Bullard, Mary E........117
Burke, Arvin S.......... 82
" Eliza A.......... 82

Burke, James M.......... 82
" Jessie G.......... 82
" Mervin H......... 82
" Myrtie M......... 82
Burns, Abel M.......... 82
" Harrison A....... 83
" Jessie G.......... 82
" Orpha V......... 83
Burt, Arthur W..........101
" Rev. A. W...98, 100, 101
" Sophie A.......98, 100
Bushnell, J. Augusta......103

C

Cable, C. W........... . 67
" Geo. W.........232
Carr, Eliza.............196
" Una J............ 95
Carrier, Ellen..........158
Carson, Dr............. 68
Carter, Edith K......... 66
Case, Fred M..........169
" Harry I..........169
" Nellie............169
Cawley, Bertha.........127
" Ella V..........127
" Jennie N........127
" John D.........127
" Wm............127
Champion, Israel......... 34
Chaplin, Anna J.........206
" Walter..........206
Chapman, Polly M......115
Chase, Hon. Salmon P....179
Cheeseman, Ida K.......131
Church, Julia M.........104
" Sarah.........29, 33
Clark, Elisha L.......... 85
" Ellen W.......... 84
" Laura 29
" Luther A......... 84
" Mrs. M. G........172
Claxton, Kate 20
Cobb, Maria L.......... 47
Cole, Mary............. 47
" Matilda........... 37

Combs, Arthur P........219
" Louis E.........219
" Louisa..........211
" Mary E.........219
" Winfred E......219
Comstock, Temperance...109
Cone, Addison.......... 29
" Albert S......... 29
" Alice............ 20
" Alice H.......... 19
" Alice S.......... 21
" Alonzo.......... 27
" Anna S.......... 28
" Apollos.......... 28
" Aristarchus...... 29
" Ashbel 19, 24
" A. T............ 23
" Barton 28
" Benjamin.......19, 21
" Betsey........... 29
" Betsey P......... 22
" Charles.......... 21
" Charles E........ 23
" Clarissa F....... 23
" Conant.........19, 20
" Damaris.......... 29
" Daniel........... 29
" Daniel, Jr........ 19
" Darius.........21, 22
" Deborah P........ 21
" Edmond.......... 28
" Elisha..........21, 23
" Eliza............ 29
" Eliza Ann H...... 23
" Elizabeth.......19, 24
" Elizabeth S....... 28
" Ellen............ 21
" Ellen A.......... 23
" Ephraim......... 27
" Francis.......... 29
" Francis S......... 23
" Frank G......... 23
" Gabriella G....... 23
" George........21, 29
" Gerard 11, 12, 13
" Hannah......21, 24, 28

Cone, Hannah B	28	Cone, Ruth	
" Harriet T	23	" 11, 12, 13, 27, 28, 29	
" Hawley	28	" Ruth S	24
" Hiram	24	" Sally	21, 22
" Huldah	28	" Sally R	21
" Inez	23	" Sally W. M	19
" Jared	14, 27, 28, 29	" Samuel W. D	22, 24
" Jededidah	28	" Sarah, 11, 12, 21, 24, 27, 28, 29	
" Jerard	13		
" Jeremiah	19, 24	" Sarah H	20
" John	20	" Solomon	19, 21
" Joseph 12, 13, 14, 19, 20, 27		" Solomon B	22, 24
		" Rev. Spencer H	19
" Joseph S	21	" Spencer W	20
" Julius	29	" Statyra	28
" Laura C	29	" Stewart B	28
" Lucretia	24	" Theodore	19, 24
" Lucy	27, 28, 29	" Timothy	20, 21
" Lucy H	27	" William	24
" Lydia G	27	" William E	29
" Margaret S	28	" Zenas	27
" Marintha	29	Cook, Sarah E	155
" Martha	19, 20, 21, 22	Cooper, Arthur	158
" Martha S	19, 21	" Frances E	158
" Martin	19, 21	Corey, Clarinda S	234
" Mary 12, 13, 14, 19, 21, 24		" Clark A	234
		" Effie S	234
" Mary B	24, 27	" Grace A	234
" Mary S	21	" James A	234
" Matthew	11, 12, 27, 28	" Jessie	234
" Nancy	117	Cottrell, Elsie A	85
" Nehemiah	11, 12, 27, 28	" Frank A	86
" Newell	27, 28	" George W	85, 163
" Norman	29	" John	86
" Norris	22, 24	" Mary A	86
" Orville	28	" Sarah E	86
" Philena	29	Cramer, Hattie M	120
" Philip	28	" Henry	120
" Polly	28	Crosby, Mary O	129
" Prudence	20	Crosier, Harriet M	184
" Rachel P	27	Crossman, Caleb S	46
" Rebecca S	21	" Martha E	46
" Reuben	22, 24	Crowell, Catharine L	127
" Rosalthe L	23	Curtis, A. B	235
" Roxanna	21, 22	" Wm. A	235

Cutler, John............ 5
" Mary............ 5

D

Dallas, Geo. M.......... 20
Daniels, Beulah.........113
Davis, Mrs. Beulah......113
" Evren A..........201
" Harriet J.....201, 203
" Jasper.......201, 203
" Jeff..........178, 179
" Josephine A......201
Dawald, Ella A. A.......124
" Emma S........124
" Hannah S.......124
" Ida A. A........124
" John...........124
Day, Erastus............ 14
Dean, J. K.............. 68
Dick, Mary A...........189
Didama, Dr............. 69
Dinsmore, Anna M....3, 204
" John B....203, 204
" Mary E........203
Dobson, Chas. M........ 82
" Geo. B.......... 82
" Myrtie M....... 82
Donelly, Jennie.........146
" Virginia........146
Dubree, Ellen B.........126
Dudley, Arthur J........171
" Arthur L........190
" Arvilla M........170
" Betsey M..170, 171, 172
" Caroline S...188, 189
" Carroll A..........171
" Carroll E. I......170
" Carroll I. E..188, 189
" Charles C........171
" Cora E..........189
" Edwin E....188, 189
" Elizabeth S.......189
" Emma M....188, 189
" Harmony....190, 191
" Helen A.....170, 172
Dudley, Helen C........190

Dudley, Helen E.........188
" Jeanie E.........190
" John A......... 170
" Rev. John H......170
" Jonathan.........170
" Lofton L.....188, 189
" Lora M..........171
" Mary A... 189
" Mary E..........171
" Oakley D........189
" Oakley S.....188, 189
" Sarah J..........171
" Sardis...188, 190, 191
" Sophia...........170
" Una F...........189
" Wm. H......170, 171
Dunbar, Amy L........184

E

Eaton, Rev.............170
Eighme, Geo. C.........233
" Mary L........233
Elder, Corinth S......... 58
Eldredge, Harriet L...... 97
" Lyman, M. D... 97
Emerick, David W.......168
" Maladine H.....168
" Nellie 169
Emmons, David......... 21
" Mary C....... 21
Engelhardt, Prof. F. E... 67
Evans, Harriet..........197
Ewen, Charlotte R......157

F

Failing, Lerusa M....... 22
Fales, Mrs..............172
Fay, Amanda S.........235
" John..............235
Fisher, Catharine........124
" Charlotte B...232, 233
" Ella A. A........124
" Harry.......124, 232
" Herbert..........232
" Lorinda S....231, 233

Fisher, Mary L......232, 233
" Samuel W........231
" Willie............124
Fiske, Chas. A..........136
" Cornelia..........136
" Ellen S...........136
" Wm. B............136
Foote, Artemisia L.......127
" Cora E...........189
Ford, Julia B...........145
" Maggie E..........245
Fratts, Katie............126
French, Annie M........102
" Capt. H. W......102
Fuller, Addie E..........218
" Hannah........... 15
" Irad.............. 15
" Jabez............ 15
" Lydia............ 15
" Stephen.......... 15
" Thankful........ 15

G

Gaines, Julia............ 23
Gallett, Anna............ 47
" Chas. H.......... 47
" Chas. R.......... 47
" Harriet M........ 47
" Henry W......... 47
" James R......... 47
" Lydia V.......... 47
" Robert M........ 47
" Sarah........... 47
Gardner, Alice M........ 95
" De Witt......... 94
" Fanny I.........203
" Florence........204
" Lewis C........203
" Sarah S......... 94
Garlock, Sarah T........159
Gates, Adelaide W.......159
" Adaline E........156
" Adaline S........156
" Anna B..........156
" Annie S.........156
" Catharine C...158, 159

Gates, Charles C....155, 156
" Charles W.......159
" Charlotte R......157
" Christopher C....155
" Dudley........... 28
" Edward H........156
" Edward T....155, 156
" Elizabeth......... 41
" Ellen C..........158
" Emma M.........155
" Esther........... 15
" Frances E........158
" Francis A....155, 159
" Frederic.........158
" Frederick Wm. B..156
" George G....155, 157
" George W........159
" Georgie..........158
" Hannah.......... 15
" Henry I..........155
" James P..155, 158, 159
" John, Capt....... 12
" Joseph B........155
" Josephine C......159
" Josiah........... 15
" Julia J...........
    155,156,157,158,159
" Julia S.......155, 157
" Lizzie P.........156
" Lydia............ 27
" Sarah E.........155
" Sarah T.........159
" Statyra.......... 28
" Wm. C..........156
" Wm. R......155, 159
Gerstenkorn, Clara W.... 46
" Ernest...... 46
" Laura B.... 46
Gibbs, John C..........146
" Louisa..........146
" Sarah...........198
Gillen, Mrs............100
Gilmore, Gabriella....... 23
Glidden, Benjamin.......136
" Sarah J........136
Goessman, Prof.......... 67

Goodwin, Lydia A....... 23
Goodyear, Ernastine H....168
" Maladine H.....168
" Samuel A......168
Gowdy, Roxanna........224
Grant, Dr.............. 58
Green, Mary............ 15
Greenwood, Grace.......172

H

Hale, Sarah J..........172
Hall, Frances L......... 61
" Maria..............172
Hanley, Caleb.......... 11
Hannagan, Julia J........223
Harper, Maria L........ 50
Harris, Mrs.............100
Hart, Lucy............. 27
Hartt, Prof. C. F......... 60
Hawes, Mrs. Sarah A.....243
Hayes, Albert C..........222
" Edith M..........222
" Ethel J..........222
" Fannie E.........222
" Irving C.........222
Haynes, Henry S........118
" Mary A. E......118
Hazeltine, Sarah A......243
Heller, Lydia A.........126
Hewitt, Dr.............177
Hill, Eliza A............ 23
Holbrook, Rev. David....169
Holland, Dr. J. G........232
Hosmer, Rev. Stephen..6, 11
Houghton, Alice......... 19
" Joab.......... 19
Housel, John...........129
Houston, Maria Mrs......167
Humphrey, Albert N..... 50
" Asenath...49, 50
" Charles E...49, 50
" Edwin L..... 49
" Edward Y.... 50
" Ida N.....49, 50
" Susan A..... 50
Hungerford, Elizabeth... 6, 7
(17)

Hungerford, Thomas......6, 7
Huntington, Holland..... 61
" Julia M..... 59
Hurt Clara............169
" Eulalie R..........169
" Floyd............169
Hutchins, Rev. Wm......173

I

Ingham, Albert H.......167
" Albriec O......205
" Alice B........205
" Alzina A...167, 172
" Anna J....205, 206
" Anna S. 195,196,197
    198, 200, 201, 202
    203, 204, 205, 206
    207, 208.
" Arthur H.......205
" Athol W.......205
" Betsey, 167, 168, 169
    170, 171, 172.
" Betsey A.......195
" Betsey M..167, 170
" Charles D......205
" Daniel.........195
" Daniel A.......205
" Eulalie R.......169
" Fanny M..195, 201
" Fernando H.....168
" Floyd F........169
" George R......169
" Herbert W.....205
" Huldah B......167
" Ianthe I.......168
" Jean I.........204
" Jean M........205
" Julia K........205
" Latetia M......206
" Lawrence D ...195
" Lillie C........219
" Maladine H.....168
" Maria..........167
" Maria H.......167
" Mary L....195, 206

Ingham, Oscar S, 195, 204, 205, 206.
" Ossian... 195
" Ralph E. 169
" Samuel.........167
" Samuel E. 169
" Temperance S...195, 200.
" Vivian I........205
" William....167, 172
" William B..168, 169
" William S..167, 168, 169.

J

Jackson, George W......125
" Ida C..........125
" John S.........125
Jacobs, Elizabeth........147
Jenkins, Rachel P....... 27
Johnson, Daniel C....... 82
" Eliza A........ 82
" Irene........... 82
" Loraine........ 82
" Myrtie........207
Jones, Carroll W........188
" Charles W.......187
" Edna A.........188
" Elma M.........187
" Mary E..........185
Joslin, Adelaide A........206
" Audrey.........207
" Carl............207
" Clarence........207
" Cora............207
" Emery A........206
" Harry...........207
" Hattie M........207
Judson, Emily B........172

K

Kellogg, Dorastses.......168
" Maladine H....168
Kelsey, Asa Strong.......157
" Emma S.........157

Kelsey, Frank G.........157
" Joseph S........157
" Julia S..........157
" Louise J........157
Kennedy, Julia........... 205
King, Rev. Edward......231
" Edward (S.)...231, 232, 233.
" Iola A............125
" Lorinda S.....231, 232
" William..........125
Kinsey, Clara E......... 23
" J. F............ 23
Kitson, Louise J........157
Knapp, Charles C........ 83
" Edmond R......212
" Elmira A........ 83
Knapp, F. Melvin.......212
" Frankie M....... 84
" Jessie L........212
" Julia H......... 83
" Laura C........212
" Lora E.........212
" Lucia E......... 84
" Mabel 84
" Melvin S.......212
" Rupert L.......212
" Wm. W......... 83
Knox, Jennie............185

L

Law, Albert R..........222
" Jessie M..........222
Leach, Elsie S...........157
" Julia S..........157
" Lawrence L......157
" Margaret K......157
" Marshall W......157
Leet, Alexander......22, 24
" Eliza Ann......... 22
" George........... 22
" Hannah C........ 24
" Harriet 22
" James............ 24
" John............. 24
" Malvina.......... 22

Lect, Martha............ 22	March, Dr. Alden........ 62
" Mary............. 24	Marshall, Hope..........145
" Menjo............. 22	Martin, Anna, 45, 46, 47, 48, 49
" Sally C............ 22	50, 81.
" Ursula............ 24	" Anna P......... 52
Le Valley, D............. 22	" Asenath S....45, 48
" Martha........ 22	" Clark........... 45
Libby, Carrie............ 57	" John C......45, 50
Livezey, Angeline S......125	" Maria L......... 50
" Azariah S......125	" Permelia W...... 51
" Edward W......125	" Sophia S....3, 51, 81
" Ella M.........125	" Thomas 45, 51, 52, 81
" Elmer B........125	Marvin, Mr.............. 22
" Ida C...........125	" Martha.......... 22
" Iola A..........125	Matthews, Mary.........200
" Jesse L.........125	McChesney, Mr......... 100
" Joseph D.......125	McFarlane, Ann C....... 43
Logan, Mr...............175	" Clara W...... 46
" Eliza S..........116	" Hugh........ 46
" Elmer H.........116	McGhie, Charlotte B.....236
" Henry S.........116	" John..........233
" James A.........116	Meacham, Alice E.......184
" James W.........116	" Amy L........184
" John F..........116	" Asenath S., 183, 184
" Walter W........116	224.
Loomis, Eliza............ 29	" Carey L.......184
" Nathan......... 29	" Charles H.....184
Loveland, Aurelia........185	" Cleantha M....239
" Ella...........218	" Cynthia C.....184
Low, Miss...............100	" Francis W.....184
Lyman, Judge............ 99	" Franklin S....239
	" George........184
M	" Harriet........184
Mack, Col. David........311	" Harry B.......184
" Dorothy..........115	" Lawrence L.184, 224
" Elijah S.........115	" Minnie A..184, 224
" Josiah............ 11	" Parsons P...3, 183
" Sarah............ 11	239.
" Zilpah........... 55	" Sally S........239
Manier, John............ 60	" Sarah E.......239
" Julia S......... 60	" Wm. I........239
Manville, Arthur H...... 23	" Winfield D....184
" Ellen A........ 23	Mellen, Jane R..........235
" Frances E...... 23	" Joel B..........235
" Roderick...... 23	" Matilda S........235
" Roderick W.... 23	" Wm. A..........235

Merritt, Mary............128
Metcalf, Anna M......... 97
" John........93, 183
" Julia............183
" Lucina.......... 93
Miller, Emily E......... 23
" George L........ 23
" George W........ 23
" Harriet T........ 23
" Lydia A. G...... 23
" William.......... 23
Mixter, Adaline S., Mrs..156
Moore, Jean I...........204
Morehouse, Jephtha B....201
" Josephine A..201
" Mabel R.....201
Morrell, Sally W........ 19
Moulton, Chas. E........146
" Ellen L........146
" Henry M......146
" Nancy A......146
Mousehunt, Fenton......207
" George......207
" Glen........207
" Justus......207
" Sarah A.....207
Munch, Charles.........124
" Emma S.......124
Munger, Alice..........198

N

Newkirk, Tamson B......127
Newton, Alice M........186
" Ambrose........ 94
" Lucy S......... 94
Noble, Asenath...48, 49, 50
" Asenath S.....48, 49
" Charles S........ 49
" Harry S.......... 49
" James........48, 51
" James M.......... 49
" Mary B.......... 48
" Nettie B......... 49
" Thomas M........ 49
" William B........ 49
Noyes, Joseph P......... 68

O

Olmstead, Albert....220, 222
" Albert F.......220
" Albert W.....220
" Alice J.......220
" Ashbel........ 29
" Edith M......220
" Fannie A.....220
" Jennie E......220
" Julia I....220, 221
" Miranda...220, 221
" Parks........220
" Ruth C....... 29
Osborne, Mrs. Anna...... 15
" Dr............. 15
Otis, Ella M............227
" Isadore...........227
" Mary C...........227
" Wm. K., M. D.....227
" Wm. L............227
Otto, Mrs. Effie.........200

P

Palmer, Dorothy......... 15
" Florence L...... 57
" William......... 15
Parke, John............247
" Sarah S.........247
Parker, Martha B.......114
Parks, Laura............ 78
" Sarah E., Mrs..... 80
Parmalee, Betsey....... 22
Parsons, Elijah.......... 34
Pasco, Emma M......189
" Francis M........189
" Maurice D.......189
Paty, Mrs. George.......100
Payne, Emily........... 70
Pease, Sibyl.............243
Peck, Ellen............. 21
" H. A............ 21
Percival, Elizabeth...... 41
Perkenpine, Catharine....151
Perry, Effie.............200
Pettit, Emma...........186

Pettit, Lavern H........201
" Orlando W.......201
" Rosalie M.......201
" Vernon J........201
Phelps, J. H............128
" Mary............128
Pierce, Alvah B........228
" Betsey..........228
" McKendrie B.....228
Poe, Libbie.............196
Pratt, Almira S.....186, 187
" Arthur D.....186, 187
" Benjamin.........186
" Clara............186
" Edwin D..........187
" Elizabeth W......187
" Elma M..........187
" Sumner G........186
Purple, Lucinda A......119

R

Rathborne, Catharine L... 58
" Joseph....... 58
" Joseph C..... 58
Read, Alzina A..........172
" Emily E.......... 23
" Lizzie S..........180
" Rev. H. W..3, 170, 172
" Rev. W. S....... 23
Reed, Maria.............167
Remington, Hiram....... 89
" Sophia....... 89
Richmond, Sally......... 21
Robbins, Margaret S.....113
Roberts, Ellen B........137
" George H.......137
" Isabel W........137
" Joseph A.......137
" Wm. B..........137
Roe, Hannah E.......... 22
" N. H.............. 22
Rogers, Elizabeth........ 15
" John........... 15
" Mary........... 15
" Sarah...12, 13, 14, 15
" Thomas..12, 13, 14, 15

Rogers, Thomas, Jr....... 15
Root, Anna..........45, 97
" Anna M........... 97
" Anna S........96, 97
" Azariah S......96, 97
" Daniel....45, 183, 217
" Elvira............ 79
" Fanny.............217
" Francis M......... 97
" Harvey...........243
" James F........... 96
" Laura M........75, 79
" Maria D........... 75
" Mary S., Mrs........ 89
" Sally.............183
" Capt. Solomon...75, 79
" Solomon F......... 96
Rowling, Ann A......... 89
" John H........ 89

S

Sandborn, Albert R......199
" Alice B........199
" Alice L... 197, 198
" Alta A........196
" Anna M...202, 204
" Arlie B........199
" Bessie A.......197
" Betsey A...195, 196
  197, 198, 199, 200
" Blanche A.....200
" Chester E.....199
" Clara A.......199
" Claude I.......200
" Clifford L......197
" Clifton A......197
" Columbus...196, 198
  199.
" Cora A... 199
" Edna A........196
" Edward,195,200,201
" Effie O........200
" Eliza B........199
" Eliza C........196
" Elzora S.......197
" Enoch.........201

Sandborn, Ernest B.....200
" Ernest E.....197
" Eva R........200
" Fanny L......203
" Fanny M.,201, 202 203, 204.
" Freddie E.....200
" George.......200
" Harriet E.....197
" Harriet J.....203
" Harry........199
" Helen A......197
" Helen M......199
" Irvin......196, 200
" Iva B........200
" Jessie........199
" Josephine A...200 201.
" Josephine L...196
" Justus....196, 197
" Justus S..200, 201
" Lawrence.....196
" Lawrence W..199
" Libbie........196
" Libbie P......196
" Lyman N.....203
" Mary E.......203
" Mary M......200
" May B.......199
" Mehettable A..202
" Morrison..196, 200
" Norman T.,202,203
" Rosalie M.,200, 201
" Sarah G......198
" Temperance M.,196 198.
" Temperance S., 200 201.
Sanderson, Lizzie S.......180
Sargent, Eugene..........208
" Hattie A.......208
Saterlee, Alfred M.......114
" Clarence O.....114
" Hannah L......114
" Wallace B......114
" William G......114

Schaupp, Cora A........199
Schenck, Mary E........116
Schoenan, May E........203
" William H.....203
Scoles, Helen M...........199
" Rev. James W....199
Scott, Allen C...........234
" Clarence B........234
" Effie S............234
" Frederick A.......234
" Grace E...........234
" Herbert A........234
" Walter E.........234
Shailor, Hattie M........119
" Simon N........120
Sharp, Thomas R....187, 188
Shaw, Rev.............177
Sherman, Nettie B....... 49
Shoft, Elizabeth.......... 28
Sibley, Jeremiah.......... 29
" Sarah........... 29
Simpkins, Annie A....... 71
" Bertrand D.... 71
" Bessie......... 71
" Charles S...... 71
" Charles W..... 71
" Clara E........ 71
" Edgar W...... 71
" Frank M....... 71
" Leon T........ 71
" Zilpha......... 71
Silliman, Anna........... 28
Skinner, Aaron, Capt.... 12
Smith, Abby A..........113
" Abner...........113
" Abner C., 109, 145, 146 147.
" Abner R....114, 115
" Addie E.......218
" Adelaide F......147
" Albert...86, 243, 244
" Albert A........119
" Albert F........119
" Albert L......86, 244
" Albert M.....86, 244
" Alden, 3, 113, 119, 120

Smith, Alden N.........120
" Alice A., 218, 219, 245
" Alice L..........197
" Alice M..........186
" Allen M.......64, 68
" Alleta V. D......117
" Almira,......183, 186
" Amanda.....231, 235
" Ambrose, 163, 227, 228
" Ambrose O...227, 228
" Angeline..........183
" Angeline S...123, 124 125.
" Ann A........... 89
" Ann S..........222
" Anna, 41, 45, 81, 93, 96 163, 195.
" Anna A..........163
" Anna B..........190
" Anna G..........223
" Anna L.......... 60
" Anna O.......... 15
" Anna V. M......117
" Annie M..........102
" Artemisia L......127
" Arthur C........186
" Arthur L........191
" Asa..34, 163, 183, 184 185, 186, 187, 188, 189 190, 224.
" Asenath, 41, 75, 84, 183
" Asenath A....... 41
" Aulus........64, 66
" Aurelia L........185
" Azariah.34, 41, 55, 56 58, 59, 60, 61, 62, 64 65, 66, 67, 68, 69, 70 71, 75, 94, 101, 109 123, 124, 125, 126 127, 128, 129, 130, 131
" Benjamin......... 15
" Benjamin F....... 75
" Benjamin M..145, 146
" Bernard H.......245
" Bertha M........119
" Bessie E........115

Smith, Betsey...163, 167, 227 228.
" Betsey W........ 75
" Beulah D........113
" Byron C.........186
" Calvin, 33, 34, 55, 86 163, 167, 170, 183 184, 185, 186, 188 190, 195, 200, 201 204, 206, 211, 212 213, 217, 218, 219 220, 221, 222, 223 224, 227, 228, 231 234, 235, 239, 243 244, 245.
" Candace C.......145
" Carl B..........218
" Caroline.....183, 188
" Carrie..........114
" Carrie B......86, 244
" Catharine E...... 56
" Catharine L......127
" Catharine P......151
" Catharine S......147
" Charles, 56, 59, 60, 211 212.
" Charles A.......147
" Charles B.......145
" Charles H.......115
" Charles M........ 78
" Charles N....222, 223
" Charles S......76, 78
" Clara..........64, 69
" Clara I..........147
" Clara S......86, 244
" Clarence E.......218
" Clarence H......185
" Clarinda......231, 234
" Clarissa A....227, 228
" Clarkson.184, 217, 224
" Clayton O........224
" Clifford I........198
" Clifton E........198
" Clinton J........198
" Corinth.........211
" Corinth S......58, 59

Smith, Cynthia..211, 213, 214
" Daisy W.......... 60
" Daniel........... 61
" Daniel W........ 89
" Diodate.......... 15
" Dorothy...15, 113, 115
" Dullas........... 64
" Dwight..........218
" Dwight I........219
" Dwight N........185
" Ebenezer, 86, 163, 219
220, 243, 244, 245.
" Edith K.......... 66
" Edith M.........191
" Edson 243
" Edward C.....98, 105
" Edward E........119
" Edward L....124, 126
" Edward P.....94, 104
" Edward S........126
" Edwin....219, 220, 243
245.
" Edwin D.........185
" Edwin H......86, 244
" Edwin R.......... 96
" Effie L..........279
" Electa..........217, 223
" Electa W.........145
" Eliphalet 15
" Eliza...... 5, 75, 81
" Eliza A........76, 77
" Eliza S..........116
" Elizabeth..6, 14, 29, 33
34, 37, 41.
" Elizabeth B.......124
" Elizabeth J.......147
" Ella F........86, 244
" Ella L............218
" Ella V...........127
" Ellen B...........126
" Elma M......212, 213
" Elmira W........ 75
" Elsie B..........118
" Elvira 79
" Emily L..........105
" Emma............ 76

Smith, Emma L..........186
" Emma P..........186
" Erastus......109, 151
" Ernest B......... 95
" Estella..........198
" Estella M........224
" Esther........... 15
" Esther L.........119
" Eugene L........115
" Eugene O........222
" Eva S...........126
" Eveline C....147, 151
" Eveline C. B......117
" Fannie E........224
" Fannie R., 218, 220, 245
" Fanny............217
" Fanny R..........217
" Flora Lena........245
" Florence A.......127
" Florence E........102
" Florence M.......118
" Frances L......... 61
" Frank E......115, 185
" Frank R..........127
" Frank W.....185, 186
" Franklin..217, 222, 223
" Fred B..........115
" Frederic W.......119
" Frederick B...123, 127
" Gad.....113, 117, 118
" George......183, 190
" George A........118
" George C.........147
" George E........191
" Gerald B......... 98
" Gertrude B......104
" Grace T.......... 95
" Gurdon B......... 66
" Hannah.........5, 15
" Hannah G........ 15
" Hannah L....113, 114
" Hannah S........124
" Harmony 183, 190
" Harriet....64, 65, 183
" Harriet L..97, 212, 213
" Harriet M........184

Smith, Harriet N.........119
"   Harriet V.........113
"   Harry E..........185
"   Hattie E.... 186
"   Hattie M.....119, 198
"   Helen M.......... 76
"   Henry....113, 115, 211, 227.
"   Henry F..........118
"   Henry W.........244
"   Herbert C........191
"   Herbert H... 60
"   Herbert Wendell..186
"   Hope M..........145
"   Horace P.........115
"   Hosea B.......... 95
"   Howard 243, 245
"   Ida B.............118
"   Ida L............127
"   Isaac A......123, 127
"   James 94
"   James L..........114
"   James O.......... 89
"   Jane 5, 217, 223
"   Jennie D.........146
"   Jennie K.........185
"   Jennie M.........120
"   Jennie N.........127
"   Jeremiah 1st....33, 34, 109, 113, 115, 117, 119, 120, 123, 127, 128, 129, 130, 135, 141, 145, 146, 147, 151, 155, 157, 158, 159.
"   Jeremiah 2d...109, 113, 114, 115, 117, 118, 119, 120.
"   Jeremiah 3d...113, 114, 115.
"   Jeremiah 4th.......113
"   Jeremiah 5th......114
"   Jeremiah J........118
"   Jeremiah W.......117
"   Jerome 185
"   Jerusha Augusta...103

Smith, Jessie M...185, 222, 223
"   John..5, 41, 51, 75, 79, 80, 81, 223.
"   John Calvin..55, 56, 57, 58.
"   John H.......... 80
"   John M...93, 97, 98, 163
"   Jonah............ 15
"   Joseph..41, 89, 94, 102
"   Joseph A.........146
"   Josephine P......147
"   Judson.........94, 103
"   Julia.........217, 221
"   Julia B......145, 191
"   Julia J..109, 155, 223
"   Julia L............218
"   Julia M....59, 104, 183
"   Julia S........60, 145
"   Justus B..........218
"   Kate W.......... 98
"   Katie F..........126
"   Kirby W..........191
"   Larissa M.....123, 130
"   Laura C......211, 212
"   Laura P........78, 79
"   Lawrence..211, 212, 213
"   Leslie............218
"   Leslie B..........127
"   Leslie C..........219
"   Lofton J......185, 186
"   Lorinda...........231
"   Louis C........98, 222
"   Louisa..56, 64, 69, 145, 146, 217, 221, 223
"   Louisa C..........211
"   Louisa W.........212
"   Lucina 93
"   Lucinda A....119, 120
"   Lucy..........93, 94
"   Lucy E...........118
"   Ludlow........64, 70
"   Lulu B...........185
"   Lydia......14, 15, 24
"   Lydia A.........126
"   Lyman E.220, 243, 245
"   Mabel E..........198

(18)

Smith, Mabel O..........130
" Maggie E..........245
" Margaret A.......104
" Margaret S...113, 114
" Maria............211
" Maria D.......... 75
" Maria E..........145
" Marie E..........146
" Marinda L........115
" Marshall F.......118
" Martha...........243
" Martha B.........114
" Martha L.........119
" Mary...6, 7, 14, 15, 19 27, 56, 64.
" Mary A...........114
" Mary Ann,75,80,86,244
" Mary A. E........118
" Mary B......219, 245
" Mary C.......104, 227
" Mary E..116, 117, 185 218, 219, 245.
" Mary G.......... 15
" Mary M.......95, 128
" Mary O..........129
" Mary P..........128
" Mary S......89, 218
" Matilda......231, 235
" Matthew.........3, 15
" Matthew 1st......3, 5
" Matthew 2d......5, 11
" Matthew 3d...5, 11, 15 19, 24, 27, 29, 30, 33
" Matthew 4th....3, 6, 7 11, 12, 14, 15, 19, 21 22, 23, 24, 27, 28, 29 30, 33, 34, 37, 41, 109 163, 247.
" Matthew 5th..3, 11, 12 13, 14, 29, 33, 34, 37 41, 45, 55, 75, 86, 89 93, 109, 113, 123, 135 141, 145,151,155, 163 167,183,195,211, 217 227,231,239, 243, 244 247.

Smith, Matthew 6th...33, 34 41, 45, 48, 49, 51, 55 56, 58, 59, 61, 70, 75 79, 81, 84, 85, 86, 89 93, 94, 95, 96, 97, 101 102, 103, 104, 163 244.
" Matthew 7th....41, 51 75, 76, 77, 78, 79, 80 81, 82, 83, 84, 85, 86 244.
" Matthew 8th....75, 76 77, 78.
" Matthew 9th...... 76
" Maud H..........186
" Maurice B........104
" Milton...217, 218, 219 220, 245.
" Minnie A.....184, 224
" Miranda......217, 220
" Morgan...........243
" Nancy.......118, 227
" Nancy A......145, 146 151, 227.
" Nancy C.....117, 118
" Nathaniel R..113, 114
" Nellie...........114
" Nelson.......123, 128
" Nettie S..........117
" Newton........64, 68
" Obadiah..163, 231,232 233, 234, 235.
" Olive............ 15
" Oliver...123, 129, 163 184, 217, 218, 219 220, 221, 222, 223 224, 245.
" Oliver C.....130, 224
" Orrin.163, 211,212,213
" Parks............ 78
" Percy C.......... 96
" Percy L........95, 96
" Philip M.........105
" Polly M..........115
" Rebecca R........124
" Robbins T....145, 147

Smith, Robert M.... 105, 147
" Rosina............243
" Rosina M.........245
" Roxanna G.......224
" Rupert V. D......102
" Ruth......14, 27, 123
" Ruthy............123
" Sallie S...........126
" Sally..75, 85, 163, 239
" Sally R...........183
" Sally W..........211
" Samuel....3, 5, 15, 41
    51, 93, 94, 95, 96, 97
    98, 101, 102, 103, 104
" Samuel E......... 98
" Sarah....11, 14, 15, 29
    33, 34, 93, 94, 211
    247.
" Sarah A...........243
" Sarah B......124, 126
" Sarah E.......... 80
" Sarah S......211, 212
" Sereno.......123, 128
" Seviah T..........231
" Sibyl P.......... 243
" Sophia...51, 80, 81, 89
    109, 123, 130, 141.
" Sophia E......80, 101
" Sophia W......... 89
" Sophie A......... 98
" Susanna....14, 30, 124
    125.
" Sylvester..........163
" Tamson B........127
" Temperance...109, 113
    135, 163.
" Temperance A.113, 120
" Temperance C.109, 145
" Thankful.......... 15
" Theodore C........102
" Theodore W...... 98
" Thomas..3, 6, 7, 12, 13
    14, 15.
" Una J............ 95
" Virginia D........146
" Walter A.........191

Smith, Walter C.........186
" Walter M.........147
" Walter S....64, 67, 68
" Wayland.........217
" Wayland F.... ...218
" William 243
" William A........223
" William E........151
" William G........118
" William M..56, 61, 64
    65, 66, 67, 68, 69, 70
" William S....124, 126
" William W.......118
" Winfred E....219, 245
" Zilpah............ 55
" Zilpha..56, 64, 70, 217
    224.
" Zilpha A......... 59
Sneyd, Catharine S.......147
Sparks, Jonas............ 15
Sparks, Olive............ 15
Sparrow, Alice.......... 20
" Mr............. 20
Spencer, Ann...........222
" Elias T......... 81
" Eliza.....81, 82, 83
" Eliza A......81, 82
" Elmira A.....81, 83
" Joseph, M. D....20
" Julia H......81, 83
" Lucy F......81, 83
" Martha......... 19
" Mary.......... 21
" Rebecca........ 21
" Ruth........... 24
" William........ 7
Spinner, F. E............179
Stanton, Eliza A......... 77
" Emroy E....... 78
" Fred P.........213
" Harriet L.......213
" Helen L.......213
" Henry E........ 77
" Luke W........ 78
" Robert H....... 78
Steele, Annie..............156

Steelman, Angeline......123
Stevens, Elizabeth........189
Stevenson, Chas. A....... 20
Stewart, Chas. E......... 23
" Clara E......... 23
" Clarissa F....... 23
" Elisha M........ 23
" Harriet A........ 23
" James W....... 23
" Jennie F........ 23
" Julia G......... 23
" William J....... 23
Storm, Azariah S........ 70
" Bertrand.......70, 71
" Catharine E...... 56
" Clara E........70, 71
" Emily P......... 70
" Emily Z......... 71
" James B. B....... 70
" Katie K.......... 71
" Lyman P......... 71
" Mack P.......... 71
" Mary P.......... 71
" Walter........... 70
" Walter L......... 70
" Zilpha......... 70, 71
Strickland, Edna L.......130
" Larissa M.....130
" Marquis L....130
Stringer, Clara........86, 244
Strong, Rev. A. K....... 59
" Asenath.......... 84
" Elisha........84, 221
" Ellen W......... 84
" Louisa S........221
" Susan........... 37
Sumner, Gen. E. V......174
Sweet, Renetta.......... 57
Swinburne, Dr..........178

T

Tappan, Prof. H. B...... 56
" Rev. Wm. B..... 61
Taylor, Sarah J.... 171
Thompson, Charles C.....228

Thompson, Chas. G......228
" Clarissa A.....228
" Henry S......228
" Lora C.......228
Tower, Seviah...........231
Tracy, Daniel........... 30
" Eliphalet......... 30
" Elizabeth......... 30
" Eveline C........151
" Gamaliel R....... 30
" Hannah S........ 30
" Jedediah......... 30
" Jerusha.......... 30
" Nehemiah....12, 13, 14
  30.
" Rachel........... 30
" Sarah............ 30
" Susanna, 12, 13, 14, 30
" Tryphena......... 30
" William H........151
Traviss, Andrew.....197, 199
" Bessie E........197
" Clara A.........199
" Clifton A.......197
" Elzora S........197
Tripp, Hattie L........... 64
" Lewis S.......... 64
" Zilpha S.......... 64
Trowbridge, Harriet N....119
Tully, Wm., M. D....... 62
Tyler, Erastus H.........136
" Eveline H........136
" Sarah J..........136
" Wm. H.......... 62

V

Van Duyn, Dr........... 68
Van Duzer, Sophia E.....101
Van Schaack, Albione L.. 57
" Calvin...... 57
" Carrie L.... 57
" Catharine L. 56
  58.
" Cornelius P. 56
  57.

Van Schaack, Florence L.. 57
" Henry C. 56, 57
" John C..... 57
" Louisa S..56, 58
" Peter ...56, 57
" Renetta S... 57
" Robert C... 57
" Robert H.56, 57
Vibert, Amy H..........120
Voltz, Bertha A.........125
" Edward L. S........125
" John M............125
" Susanna S..........125
" Wm. T. L..........125

W

Wadhams, Myrtic M...... 82
" Truman H..... 82
Wakefield, Elizabeth......187
Walker, Anna B.........190
" Charles H.......126
" Sarah B.........126
Ward, Betsey............. 75
Warner, Electa..........145
Warren, Francis E....... 76
" Fred E......... 77
" Helen F........ 77
" Helen M........ 76
Watson, Frances E....... 23
Wattles, Sophia.......... 89
Weld, Alice M..........198
" Elmer D..........198
" Evren A..........198
" Temperance M.....198
" Willard...........198

Wells, Alice M.......... 47
" Ann C.........45, 46
" Anna....45, 46, 47, 48
" Blanche.......... 47
" Caroline A.....45, 46
" Elisha A......... 45
" Henry C......45, 48
" Horace E...45, 47, 48
" Horace L......... 47
" Jane C........45, 48
" Julia W.......... 47
" Leila A 48
" Lemuel M......45, 47
" Lydia V.......45, 47
" Maria L.......... 47
" Martha E.....45, 46
" Mary A........45, 48
" Mary C.......... 47
Weston, Julia W......... 47
Wheat, Permelia......... 51
Williams, Elsie B........118
Witherell, Adelaide......159
Woods, Clinton E........ 50
" Florence E....... 50
" Ida N 50
Woodworth, Henry P....202
" Isabelle B...202
" Lucy I......202
Wright, Charles......... 85
" Elsie A 85
" Helen M....... 85
" Louisa.........212
" Rev 173
" Sally 85
" Wm. S......... 85
Wylie, Lora M..........171

www.ingramcontent.com/pod-product-compliance
Lightning Source LLC
Chambersburg PA
CBHW031954230426
43672CB00010B/2143